Wagadu
Vol 16

Wagadu
Vol 16

A Journal of Transnational Women's and Gender Studies

Nikita Dhawan

To order additional copies of this book, contact:
Xlibris
1-888-795-4274
www.Xlibris.com
Orders@Xlibris.com
543388

Editorial Team

TABLE OF CONTENTS

BOOK REVIEWS

Wagadu, Journal of Transnational Women's and Gender Studies

SPECIAL ISSUE

Difference that makes no Difference:

The Non-Performativity of Intersectionality and Diversity

ONE

HOW NOT TO DO THINGS WITH WORDS

Sara Ahmed
Goldsmiths, University of London

Correspondence: Sara Ahmed, Goldsmiths, University of London S.Ahmed@gold.ac.uk

I first used the word "non-performativity" at a workshop on racism in higher education that took place at Leeds University in 2002. It popped right out of my mouth when I was asking a question. I am sure it came out like that because it gave expression to a sentiment that was being shared by many of us in the room. We were discussing how easy it was for universities to commit to anti-racism without doing anything that provided evidence of that commitment. Even saying this is saying something: it implies a commitment can be given *in order to* provide evidence of something. I will return to why and how evidence matters in due course. And the word that came to mind for an action that was not followed through was "non-performative." A commitment is often understood as a performative: it is not describing or denoting something; a commitment "commits." But what seemed to be the case was that commitments were makeable *because* they were not doable: it seems you can make a commitment because commitments do not commit institutions to a course of action. Commitments might even become a way of not doing something by appearing to do something.

Understanding the role or function of institutional commitments was to understand how institutions do not do things with words, or how institutions use words as a way of not doing things. I often wonder if there is an instruction manual somewhere with this as an unofficial title: *Diversity, or how not to do things with words.*

The idea that "not doing something" could be an unofficial instruction manual is suggestive. Not doing something is still an action; it might even be a technique that is perfected over time. The action being performed is just not the action made explicit by the utterance. So a commitment is still doing something even when it is not committing something.

How can not doing something be an action? Many actions might be necessary in order for something not to be done or for an attempt to transform something not to lead to a transformation of something. And the reproduction of an existing order might depend on the failure to modify that order. Reading through the papers for this special issue is like being given an object lesson in how much the reproduction of a world depends upon the containment of our efforts to transform worlds. We learn how easily diversity can be adopted by an institution as a word, or even as a motto of a city, as Shana Almeida explores in her analysis of Toronto, or as a style of leadership or management, as Mechthild Nagel discusses, with the implied intonation of diversity as civility, as getting on or getting along. We can, as Eike Marten does, tell the story of words like diversity as a story of usage as well as travel, how some words might be used more the more they imply something has been overcome. Policies can be adopted, words can be uttered; decisions can be made, without anything really changing. Sometimes we refer to this as the "lip service" model of diversity. To use a word like "non-performativity" is to reveal something about institutional mechanics: how things are reproduced by the very appearance of being transformed.

So, for me, using the term *non-performativity* was itself a performative utterance: I was doing something, or trying to do something, and not just say something, about how institutions can reproduce themselves at the very moments they appear not to be reproducing themselves: how diversity can be about how whiteness reappears, for instance. So it is important for me to state that I first used this word non-performativity *before* doing the empirical project on diversity work in higher education, which I draw on in my book *On Being Included: Racism and Diversity in Institutional Life* (2012). And by talking to diversity practitioners, I began to think more explicitly about the consequences of non-performativity for our own work as diversity workers; whether we are employed as practitioners or academics or are both. If institutions do words not to do things, then we have work to do, which often means work to do on these words – work to do with these words. I think my arguments in *On Being Included* were really about this: the consequences of non-performativity.

We need to recognise that even the words we use can be ways of not doing things – we are complicit and compromised because of where we work. We are not outside the institutions we are trying to transform even when we are perceived as outsiders. And so: we fight for words that keep alive certain histories, histories of struggle that were necessary for some of us to get here, to be here, knowing they will go into more general circulation and that they will lose something along the way. Following Vanessa Eileen Thompson and Veronika Zablotsky we might consider how the rhetoric of diversity can work as a distraction, how we need to reanimate words such as diversity and difference by linking them with social justice. We then are trying to modify the context in which the utterance is made. We are trying to contest the ease of a co-option. So much effort is required because of that ease, as well as to make sense of that ease. Diversity work in a more substantive sense, transforming the norms that govern institutional life, is about trying to make things more difficult than they appear to be. When words do not do something, we have to work *on* these words in order to try to *make them do something*. We have work to do because of what they do not do. I learnt from my interviews that even non-performative speech acts can be useful: if organisations are saying what they are doing, we can show they are not doing what they are saying. Diversity work often takes place in the gap between words and deeds.

We also learn that even our own words can be used to minimise the disruption cause by our efforts. But as Jane Chin Davidson reminds, we should not be silenced by what happens to our own words; speaking can be another kind of dissent, especially when you speak with a voice or an accent that makes you sound out of tune or out of place. Words like intersectionality too, words that have functioned as black feminist tools, which are sharpened when used with precision, can become non-performatives: they can circulate because they have been emptied of force; the more they move around, often by being cut off from a labouring body, the less work they do. Indeed, intersectionality can be said in order not to be done, as if saying it is doing it, almost as if the word takes the place of something, as promising more than it can deliver as Nikita Dhawan and Maria do Mar Castro suggest. Indeed, a number of papers in this special issue refer to Sirma Bilge's (2013) important critique of the "whitening" of intersectionality within European Gender studies and beyond. Bilge's exemplary work shows us how high the political stakes are; she exposes the political costs of what I called non-performativity.

To make these critiques is not to stop using the words. Words are tools. We have to use the tools that are handy. But we have a struggle on our hands because of what the words do not do. And by words we mean worlds. And by worlds we mean walls. We come up against walls because we are trying to transform institutions. Walls came up a lot in the data I collected for my research project, which involved interviewing practitioners about their work. One practitioner describes her work thus: "it's a banging your head against the brick wall job." A job description can become a wall description. My arguments about non-performativity were not just calls for action but a recognition of the collective labour that is necessary because of how institutional walls *keep standing*.

Let me explain a little more by returning to one of the examples first shared in chapter 4 of *On Being Included: Racism and Diversity in Institutional Life* (2012) on commitment. It is an example of what I have since called "wall encounters."

> When I was first here there was a policy that you had to have three people on every panel who had been diversity trained. But then there was a decision early on when I was here, that it should be everybody, all panel members, at least internal people. They took that decision at the equality and diversity committee which several members of SMT were present at. But then the director of Human Resources found out about it and decided we didn't have the resources to support it, and it went to Council with that taken out and Council were told that they were happy to have just three members, only a person on Council who was an external member of the diversity committee went ballistic – and I am not kidding went ballistic – and said the minutes didn't reflect what had happened in the meeting because the minutes said the decision was different to what actually happened (and I didn't take the minutes by the way). And so they had to take it through and reverse it. And the Council decision was that all people should be trained. And despite that I have then sat in meetings where they have just continued saying that it has to be just 3 people on the panel. And I said but no Council changed their view and I can give you the minutes and they just look at me as if I am saying something really stupid, this went on for ages, even though the Council minutes definitely said all panel members should be trained. And to be honest sometimes you just give up (2012, pp. 124-125).

So what is going on here? A lot is going on here: *what goes on involves many goings on*. We learn that even when nothing happens, nothing changes, a lot work is going on; a lot of effort, the effort to change something, the effort not to be changed by something. In the first instance, it seems as if there is an institutional decision. That is not really the first instance: there is a history of how this decision was made, how it began as a proposal. But once made, that is not the end of the story. The non-performative: it is not the end of the story. Individuals within the institution must act as if the decision has been made for it to be made. If they do not, it has not. A decision made in the present about the future, a decision that is willed, that operates under the promissory sign "we will," is overridden by the momentum of the past. In this case, the head of personnel did not need to take the decision out of the minutes for the decision not to bring something into effect. This is what I intended to reveal by calling this dynamic "non-performativity": how naming something does not bring something into effect, or how something is named *in order not to bring something into effect*. An institution can say "yes" when there is not enough behind that "yes" for something to be brought about. An institutional wall is when a will, "a yes," does not bring something about, "a yes" that conceals this "not bringing" under the appearance of "having brought."

It is only the practical effort to bring about transformation that *allows the wall to be apparent*. To those who do not come against it, the wall does not appear: the institution is experienced as "yes" as open, committed and diverse, as happy as its mission statement, as willing as its equality statement.

We are learning how institutional statements and policies are a way of not doing something. Sometimes a policy can be used as evidence: a way of saying, or of showing, that something has been done. As another practitioner I interviewed put it: "Well I think in terms of the policies, people's views are 'well we've got them now so that's done, it's finished.'....*I'm not sure if that's even worse than having nothing*, that idea in people's heads that we've done race, when we very clearly haven't done race." Policies can function as claims to performativity: as if having a policy means the work has been finished. A policy: how not to "do race" by appearing to have "done race."

The wall: that which keeps standing. By talking to diversity workers I began to appreciate how the institution is a plumbing system: you have to *work out* where the blockage is, what prevents something from moving through the system. This is why I call diversity workers "institutional plumbers." In the example from my research what stopped something from happening *could have been* the removal of the policy from the minutes; it *could have been* the failure to notice this removal; but it wasn't. It was the way in which those within the institution acted as if this policy had not been approved. A lot can be happening to stop something from happening. Let me summarise the finding: what stops movement moves.

Diversity work is hard in the sense of difficult: it requires more effort to come up against what keeps standing. The brick wall is hard in other senses too. In physics hardness refers to *the resistance of materials to change under force*. A wall, and I am thinking of an actual wall here, is made out of hard material. Say you throw something against the wall: a little object. You can witness the hardness of the wall by what happens to what is thrown: a wall might be scratched at the surface by encountering such an object. The object might splinter and break by the force of what it comes up against.

This is what diversity work sometimes feels like: scratching at the surface, scratching the surface. Hardness here is a quality of things that is revealed as an encounter between things. Diversity work is certainly an encounter between things: our bodies can be the little objects hurled against walls, those sedimented histories. Watch what happens. Ouch. And maybe it happens, time and time again. Hardness has a history or even is a history. When I say I come up against a wall I am describing what I encounter when I try to change something that has becoming harder or hardened over time. Literally I mean: when we talk about walls we are talking about the *material resistance* to being changed by force. *The materiality of resistance to transformation*: diversity workers know this materiality very well. We live this materiality.

When we use the expression "it is a banging our head against a brick wall job" it is important to recognise that the brick wall being referred to is a metaphorical wall. It is not that there "really" is a wall; it is not a physical or actual wall. That the wall is not an actual wall makes the wall even harder. The wall is a wall that might as well be there, because the effects of what is there are *just like* the effects of a wall. And yet not: if an actual wall was there, we would all be able to see the wall, or to touch it. The wall would be evidence. Yes I am back to the question of evidence: this time the wall as evidence of what a commitment does not do; the wall is evidence of the non-performative. But of course then: the wall is what does not materialize. To come up against institutional walls is to come up against what others do not see; and (this is even harder) you come up against what others are often invested in not seeing. So: the example of the diversity policy that does not do anything is a tantalisingly tangible example of what goes on so much and so often. We have many such tangible stories in this special issue. But that it is tangible, that I can share the story with you, is a consequence of diversity work and of the labour of a diversity worker, of her blood, sweat and tears. I used to think that as a researcher I was generating data on diversity work, but I have come to realise diversity work generates data.

We are telling stories about how what appears can conceal a disappearance. A policy disappears despite there being a paper trail, despite the evidence, or even because of the evidence. The paper provides evidence of a commitment. You can wave it in front of them, and it still does not appear! And there is more to say about what or who does not appear. People disappear too, because of what they make evident, of what they try to bring into view. What happened to that policy can happen to those who try to transform institutions: even if you are not asked to leave, they can make it difficult for you to keep going, to keep doing the work you are doing. The story of how the wall that keeps standing is thus the same story as the story of the exhaustion of a diversity worker, of what happens to her. In a conversation I had with diversity practitioners in 2013 a wall becomes a water canon: "It's like water cannons. Sometimes the success story is to stay standing in the face of everything they throw at you. It doesn't always feel like a success. But it is a success." The effort becomes: to stay standing.

And to stay standing in the face of what is thrown at you is an achievement. This achievement is not tangible to others. So we could say: a wall is how a wall is not revealed. Intangibility, what does not become evidence, is itself achieved. A wall that is something tangible to some is not even there for others because of who they are or because of what they are not trying to do. Those who don't come up against walls might then (do then) experience those who speak about walls as *wall makers*, as if to speak of walls is to bring something into existence that would otherwise not be there. The feminist killjoy is a wall maker. Just recall the words of the diversity practitioner: "they just look at me as if I am saying something really stupid." We can imagine the eyes rolling when she points out the policy. The diversity worker could thus be described as an institutional killjoy. I became interested in this figure of the killjoy, I began to pick her up and put her to work, after listening to another diversity practitioner. She said: "you know you go through that in these sorts of jobs where you go to say something and you can just see people going 'oh here she goes.'" We both laughed, recognizing that each other recognized that scene. It is interesting to me, on reflection, that it can be others who put into words something you have yourself have experienced. A killjoy: so often she borrows her words from others. So yes, we both recognized that each other recognized that scene.

The diversity worker in becoming an institutional killjoy is not heard; when she speaks of walls, walls come up. A wall comes up in this reframing of walls as *immaterial,* as phantoms, as how we *stop ourselves* how we stop ourselves from doing something, from being something. This means that: what is real, what is in concrete terms the *hardest,* is not always available as an object that can be perceived (from some viewing points), or an object that can be touched (even by those who are seated at the same table). *What is the hardest for some does not even exist for others.*

Special issues such as this one allow us to share our experiences of coming up against walls. These are not just depressing experiences; though depression and exhaustion are part of the story. We know so much about institutions from our own efforts to transform them. We become more creative and inventive because of how many paths are blocked. We have to find other ways of getting through. Indeed, diversity work might also require a support system: so that a diversity worker is not so exhausted by the work that she ends up giving up. We have to find ways of sharing the costs of doing this work. This is why it is so important not only to keep reflecting on our work but to keep sharing these reflections.

References

Ahmed, Sara. (2012). *On being included: Racism and diversity in institutional life.* Durham, NC: Duke University Press.

Bilge, Sirma. (2013). Intersectionality undone: Saving intersectionality from feminist intersectionality studies. *Du Bois Review: Social Science Research on Race*, 10(2), 405-424.

TWO

"WHAT DIFFERENCE DOES DIFFERENCE MAKE?": DIVERSITY, INTERSECTIONALITY, AND TRANSNATIONAL FEMINIST POLITICS

Nikita Dhawan
Universität Innsbruck
and Maria do Mar Castro Varela
Alice Salomon Hochschule Berlin

Correspondence:
Nikita Dhawan, University of Innsbruck[1] and Maria do Mar Castro Varela,
Alice Salomon University of Applied Sciences, Berlin
Nikita.dhawan@uibk.ac.at; castro@ash-berlin.eu

---

1   Nikita Dhawan would like to thank Anna Millan for her support in
    preparing the manuscript and Joanna James for her support in preparing
    this chapter

Abstract:

This paper engages with the formative concepts of diversity and intersectionality, inquiring how far they are employed as tools for achieving (gender) justice that open up spaces for marginalized constituencies, including racial and religious minorities, colonial subjects, queers, and women and how they unwittingly reify the hegemony of an entitled majority by failing to realize their emancipatory possibilities.

Intersectionality as corrective methodology

"What I find revealing in debates on intersectionality, even among its critics, is the total lack of engagement with literature outside the Euro-North American (at most Australia)." (Menon, 2015, p. 11)

The pursuit of justice has been at the heart of feminist theory and practice. The aim was and is to examine the role of gender in processes of material exploitation and epistemic violence as well as to outline strategies that enable gender equality and access to and control over resources, thereby empowering the agency of disenfranchised individuals and communities. Moreover, the effort is to enable participation of vulnerable female citizens in social and political institutions, which are responsible for and accountable to them. Contemporary discourses on (gender) justice seek to address multiple aspects including theoretical discussions of agency, autonomy, and capabilities; political questions involving participation, rights, democratization, and citizenship; economic policies about access to and control over resources; issues of cultural politics and representation; discussions in the field of law about judicial reform; and practical matters of access to redress. Debates on justice are increasingly employing the model of intersectionality, which outlines how different forms of discrimination co-constitute each other, thereby producing particular conjunctures of vulnerability and inequality. Furthermore, the production of injustice is located in a range of interconnected socio-political institutions like the heteronormative family, the community, the market, and the state.

Against this background, our paper engages with the formative concepts of diversity and intersectionality, inquiring how far they are tools for achieving (gender) justice that open up spaces for marginalized constituencies, including racial and religious minorities, colonial subjects, queers, and women and how they unwittingly reify the hegemony of an entitled majority by failing to realize their emancipatory possibilities. We take inspiration from the postcolonial feminist Sara Ahmed (2006), who argues that the diversity and intersectionality boom is for the most part "non-performative," in that it promises much more than it actually delivers. This contribution outlines the prospects and limitations of intersectionality and diversity politics, by taking a step back and assessing what has been gained through these interventions, and where it has failed. As intersectionality and diversity are often discussed together, we focus on how these are mobilized in academic discourses and beyond and their strengths and limits. The text begins by engaging with the important contribution made by diversity and intersectionality discourses and outlines how these have enriched struggles for justice. Thereafter, we take a critical look at both approaches. Here we particularly focus on interventions from the global South, which are mostly disregarded within the Western debates on intersectionality and diversity politics. Finally, we argue that despite the critique, one cannot not want diversity politics and intersectional analysis, even as it is imperative to persistently question and be vigilant about the instrumentalization of these progressive tools by hegemonic discourses and structures to sustain the status quo.

Intersectionality and Diversity: Old wines, new bottles?

Whenever intersectionality and diversity are up for debate, one is often confronted with the question: What's new about this approach? This is certainly not without good reason given that, as it has been rightly pointed out, they deal with forms and dynamics of discrimination that feminist theory and practice has been continuously reflecting upon and negotiating for over two decades. Perspectives may vary, yet the meticulous scrutiny of multiple facets of discrimination has always been a key feminist concern. At the same time, it is widely accepted that although all women experience discrimination on the basis of gender, they are not discriminated in the same way and degree. Even a cursory look at the second-wave feminist movement in the US in the 1970s reveals that with its sole focus on gender, it was already subjected to vehement critique for its racism and class bias. Various social and resistance movements (for example, the Black and lesbian movement) pointed out that categories such as race, sexuality, class, religion, and so forth were not sufficiently taken into account in white feminist scholarship and advocacy. This resulted in an epistemological framework and theoretical categories that did not adequately reflect the experiences of different subject positions. The oft-quoted statement by the Combahee River Collective astutely indicts this oversight: "A combined anti-racist and anti-sexist position drew us together initially, and as we developed politically we addressed ourselves to heterosexism and economic oppression under capitalism" (Combahee River Collective, 1984[1978], p.4). The assumption that *all* women were equally victimized by a global patriarchy was central to the critique. Such a viewpoint, which basically sums up the focus of the second-wave feminist movement, not only implies that all other power relations – such as racism and classism derive from patriarchy and correspondingly disappear with the victory over the same, but also suggest that sexism is a universal and transhistorical phenomenon. The U.S. feminists of color provided theoretical alternatives, in that they challenged the exclusive focus on a universal patriarchy that neglected other forms of discrimination (cf. Anzaldúa/Moraga, 1981; Lorde, 1984; Mohanty, 1984). It is important to note that the alternative was not to simply "add and stir" other grounds of discrimination to sexism; rather the interrelations of diverse forms of discrimination and co-constitution of social categories were taken into consideration. Thus quite early – at least in the U.S. – a multi-issues feminism emerged that provided a corrective for mainstream feminist theory and advocacy that had previously limited itself to merely one category, namely, gender, even as it was a very reductionist idea of gender. Marginalized women, whose experiences of discrimination could not be sufficiently captured by single-issue politics, always questioned and challenged the foundational premises of feminism, even as they refashioned the tools that have constituted the arsenal of feminist scholarship. As is well-known, the formerly enslaved women's rights activist Sojourner Truth gave a powerful statement on occasion of the women's right convention in Akron, Ohio in 1851 asking her "white sisters" "And ain't I a woman?!". To this day her intervention still inspires and informs (postcolonial) feminists supportive of an intersectional approach. Poststructuralist feminists underline another serious theoretical problem, namely, single-issue politics not only erases and hierarchizes different forms of oppression, it also essentializes gender (see for example Butler, 1990).

In light of these considerations, a critique of hegemonic feminism must necessarily adopt a historical approach; otherwise it fails to produce a differentiated analysis of gender relations. In this context, the postcolonial feminist Sara Suleri (1995, p.273) pointedly raises the tricky question of what comes first: gender or race? She thereby outlines the radical inseparability of the two structuring categories that are ultimately reflected in the gendering of race and racialization of gender. This highlights how race and gender are historically interwoven, even as different moments of oppression conflict with each other (see in this regard Trinh, 1989). Kimberlé Crenshaw, who is credited with coining the term intersectionality, explains this as follows:

> Because women of colour experience racism in ways not always the same as those experienced by men of colour and sexism in ways not always parallel to experiences of white women, antiracism and feminism are limited, even on their own terms. (Crenshaw, 1991, p. 1252).

Crenshaw, an African American legal theorist, points out that although the U.S.-American justice system safeguards the rights of women as well as of African American men, it insufficiently protects the rights of Black women. In the 19th century, Sojourner Truth emphasized precisely this aspect when calling for the voting rights of Black women at a time when this was only demanded for Black men.

These historical discussions might suggest that there is not anything absolutely new about intersectionality; rather old discourses are presented in a new package. However, this would be inaccurate as the intersectional approach does not simply smoothly insert itself into the postmodern project, which focuses on the multiplicity and fragmentary nature of social identities. Rather it offers "race/class/gender feminists" a theoretically challenging methodology, while simultaneously avoiding the pitfalls of an additive approach that still plagues many feminist analyses. One of the most significant advantages of an intersectional approach is its commitment to not only feminist theory, but also critical practice or a practice of critique. The intersectional approach not only addresses differences and heterogeneity, but also seeks to overcome the pitfalls of single-issue politics, as proposed by Black feminist scholarship (Hill Collins, 1990). Thus an analysis is attempted that takes into consideration the varied experiences of diverse constituencies without losing sight of the simultaneity, contradictions, and interdependencies of these perspectives. Intersectionality, as legal doctrine, can thus be described as a critical project that allows contemporary feminist research to carefully discern heterogeneity of standpoints and yet be politically and academically efficacious.

Diversity has a slightly different focus, namely, on the plurality of social categories. Above all diversity politics is devoted to promulgating an agenda of action, which provides political and social guidelines for anti-discrimination advocacy and equal opportunity politics. At the same time, it shares the assumption with the intersectional approach that power has multiple sources and is understood to operate dynamically within social and political arenas. Accordingly, experiences of racism, sexism, ableism, or classism cannot simply be separately considered within different fields that exist in isolation of each other. It is impossible to bring together these varied perspectives at a later point, as they actually have a reciprocal – sometimes conflicting relation to each other. For instance, African American feminists, who contested sexism in their own community while challenging hegemonic white feminism and a white patriarchy, were in turn often accused of heterosexism by lesbian African American feminists (see Lorde, 1984). What is apparent is that without an adequate consideration of the complex intersections of factors such as class, gender, race, and sexuality, anti-discrimination policies risk reinforcing essentialist identity politics. This brings about counter-productive effects. In this context

Angela Davis provocatively speaks of diversity and intersectionality as "difference that makes no difference".[2] She suggests that the presence of women or Black people in leading positions within universities, politics, or the free economy has not radically transformed social structures or gender and race relations. She points to the inefficacy of critical concepts that seem innovative within the academy, but in reality prove insufficient to facilitate social transformation. Here the key question is whether critical concepts are unable to deliver on their promises or whether hegemonic structures continually succeed in appropriating and de-radicalizing them.

Intersectionality in the Postcolony

The postcolonial theorist Anne McClintock (1995, p.5) proposes that race and gender are not simply a question of skin color or sexuality, but of exploitative sexual and economic relations and imperial servility. For slightly different reasons than intersectionality researchers, postcolonial feminists caution against reducing these complex fields to identity categories that ignores their interlocking and reciprocal character. From the standpoint of postcolonial feminists, imperialism cannot be understood without a theory of gender and race relations (cf. ibid., p. 6), for since its emergence, colonialism has represented a violent encounter of Western and pre-colonial power hierarchies entailing an opportunistic overlapping of colonial and native patriarchal ideologies. For instance, colonized women were already at a disadvantage within their communities before the establishment of the imperial rule, which gave their experience of colonial sexual and economic exploitation a different quality in contrast to that of the oppression of native men. Not only did colonized women have to deal with inequalities with regard to their "own men," but they also had to negotiate violent structures of imperial power relations – with white European men *and* women (cf. ibid.). Postcolonial feminism is an effort to address diverse

---

2   Angela Davis, *Feminism and Abolition: Theories & Practices for the 21ˢᵗ Century,* Public lecture at the Cornelia Goethe Centre for Women's and Gender Studies, Goethe-University Frankfurt on 03.12.2013.

social differences without undermining the necessary solidarity across categories in processes of decolonization. Discourses of resistance can inadvertently reinforce essentialisms and reifications, even as former margins are transformed into oppositional centers (Gates, 1992, p.303).

As a recent debate among Indian feminists demonstrates, it is not a given that the concept of intersectionality is automatically relevant in postcolonial contexts or augments transnational feminist alliance-building. The question of who ultimately profits from this approach remains contested.[3] Nivedita Menon (2015), in her contribution in the renowned journal *Economic & Political Weekly*[4] inquires whether the intersectional approach is meaningful in postcolonial contexts such as India. In doing so she initiated a robust discussion on the universal validity of feminist concepts – even when they function as critical tools. This revitalizes the crucial debate about the "politics of location" (Rich, 1986), which demands a critical contextualization of every political intervention. Even though Menon does not outright reject the concept of intersectionality, she sharply critiques its politics of reception. In her view, "[t]heory must be located, we must be alert to the spatial and temporal coordinates that suffuse all theorizing" (Menon, 2015, p. 2), so that intersectionality must be considered within the context of an academic imperialism of

---

3   Even a cursory engagement, for instance, with the German scholarship on intersectionality reveals the dominance of white, heterosexual, bourgeois German feminists, whose effort seems to be to "catch up institutionally with U.S. women's studies" (Puar, 2012, p.55). This is contrary to the Anglo-American context, wherein women of color initiated the discussions. Although we support an anti-essentialist politics of representation, it is imperative to address the following issues: How did the intersectional approach become hegemonic in Western feminist scholarship and who profits from its popularity? Is it agency-inducing for gendered subaltern subjects, in that it enables them to intervene and transform hegemonic structures? Or does the "First World" remain self-obsessed in the name of difference?

4   We are citing from *International Viewpoint*, an online socialist journal, where the text appeared simultaneous to its publication in the *EPW*.

categories. She draws attention to the dominance of concepts developed in the West, which are 'imported' into postcolonial spaces, while categories and concepts outlined by non-European intellectuals rarely travel in the opposite direction (ibid.). As previously pointed out by other authors, Menon too argues that intersectionality merely ends up being a buzzword for a long known fact. Focusing on India and the legacy of liberation struggles that among other things led to the emergence of an independent Republic of India, Menon employs several examples, like the issue of legal pluralism as well as caste politics, to insist that, on the one hand, India cannot be compared to the U.S and, on the other hand, how the co-constitution of categories has long been considered an unquestionable fact within Indian feminism. "My argument is," Menon states, "that the 'single axis framework' was never pre-dominant or unchallenged in our parts of the world" (ibid., p. 4). In her view, feminist politics in a context like India is unthinkable without the interventions of *Dalit*[5] women. She discusses how *Dalit* activists for instance, reject radical feminist categories such as "sex work," because these are unacceptable within a context where members of their community were forced into prostitution in the name of tradition. Striking a cautionary note *Dalit* scholars argue that the mobilization of the self-designation "sex work," which suggests wage labor and free choice, trivializes historical relations of coercion maintained by the hegemonic upper castes in sexually exploiting vulnerable *Dalit* women. Menon uses this example to illustrate the interplay between gender, sexuality, class and caste to suggest that it was never possible to pursue single-issue politics in India. Furthermore, she reminds us of the appropriation of the concept of intersectionality by the UN, which has not only resulted in the de-radicalization of Crenshaw's original concept, but also contributed to the de-politicization of gender studies in general. "In international human rights discourses, intersectionality helps perform the function of governmentalizing and depoliticizing gender, by assuming a pre-existing woman bearing multiple identities" (ibid, p. 9). This resonates with Gayatri Chakravorty Spivak's (2004) critique of human rights

---

5   Dalit is the self-chosen designation by groups traditionally regarded as "untouchable" in the Hindu caste system.

discourse, with which we will engage below. But before we do so, we would like to briefly outline two responses to Menon's intervention: Mary John (2015) is skeptical about the claim that Indian feminist theory has always promoted a multi-issue politics. She is moreover unconvinced that Menon's preferred strategy of destabilization of social categories would facilitate a more inclusive politics (ibid., p. 73). For John, the strength of an intersectional approach lies in its ability to make transparent the problem of multiple and overlapping discriminations "by pointing to a place where identities fail to appear or be recognized as we might have expected them" (ibid.). Here John supports the claim that intersectionality functions as a corrective methodology. John agrees with Menon on the problem of universalism and the assumption that any theory developed in the West can be applied everywhere, while non-Western concepts and theories are not guaranteed the same reception. She, however, suggests that simply rejecting all universalisms is not a viable solution:

> It is true that, given our colonial and postcolonial histories, our intellectual spaces are cluttered with false universalisms. But it is equally true that we have been trapped by false particularisms, and ever false rejections of the universal. (ibid., p. 75)

In response to the critique that the concept of intersectionality is not radically new, John reminds us that Crenshaw never claimed this in the first place; rather Crenshaw always located her concept in the collective history of Black feminism in the US. Finally, Meena Gopal (2015) adds that Menon presents a very selective description of the Indian feminist movement and neglects the category of "class," a common problem in contemporary feminist politics. Despite their differences, all the interlocutors agree that a discussion on the contribution of intersectionality in revitalizing feminist theory and politics is meaningful and fruitful. However, a simple "transplantation" from the West onto the postcolonial contexts seems questionable and intellectually dubious. But as John remarks: "Above all else, then, there is a profound need for more critical dialogue across global feminist margins and centers. I, for one, think that intersectionality would make for an excellent candidate in such an endeavor." (Menon, 2015, p.76).

Non-performativity of Diversity Politics

Despite the hype surrounding diversity as an emancipatory concept, the postcolonial feminist Sara Ahmed (2006) suggests that regrettably diversity politics mostly serves as mere lip service in academic and policy discourses. Examining institutional commitments to social change through implementation of diversity and equality programs, she identifies an effect she calls non-performativity of diversity speech. As Ahmed points out, the non-performativity of an utterance does not indicate its failure; rather its very success lies in not doing what it claims, even if it is read as performative, namely, as doing what it pledges. Although the discourses and guidelines surrounding diversity are not completely ineffective, nonetheless they do not necessarily lead to the effects they name and promise, but are still perceived as performative (Ahmed, 2006, p. 104). This generates power effects, in that the non-performativity can be applied and used strategically. The claim made by an institution or university that it is anti-racist or anti-sexist has the paradox effect, such that racism can no longer be criticized within such institutions. Immunized through the self-representation of being anti-racist and diversity-friendly, institutional racism and sexism becomes impossible to name thereby rendering discriminatory practices invisible and making them all the more difficult to contest. The effect is that the non-performative rhetoric prevents combatting that which it pretends to abolish. Ironically, anti-racist and diversity-friendly discourses can, at the same time, function as a resource for these struggles, because they enable the exposure of the gap between claim and practice. On one hand, naming and recognition of discriminatory and exclusionary structures is necessary in order to be able to even imagine equality and justice. On the other hand not every form of ritualized distancing from racist or sexist practices fosters the elimination of inequality and injustice. Ahmed states that paradoxically the more the focus on diversity management in institutions such as universities, the less diverse these institutions seem to be. This negative relation between rhetoric and reality indicates the institutional farce performed in the name of diversity politics. An excellent example of this is the proliferation of seals of approval given to institutions to certify them as diversity-friendly. For instance, several evaluations have been introduced to assess the family friendliness of universities. This is essentially part of the marketing strategy towards corporatization and neoliberalization of universities (see Brown, 2015, pp. 175), which present themselves as cosmopolitan, transnational, and diverse as these credentials influence their international ranking. However, despite claims of "doing diversity" the status quo within universities is upheld via Eurocentric and androcentric structures. The rhetoric of diversity and equality is instrumentalized in order to circumvent the accusation of racism and discrimination. At the same time, there is a systematic resistance against the institutionalization of diversity, which would structurally entrench principles of gender and racial equality through changes in the curriculum as well as through more democratic hiring practices. Here we see the ideological function of diversity programs as legitimizing performance indicators (Ahmed, 2006). It is thus imperative to situate the "mainstreaming" of intersectionality politics and diversity management within the historical and economic landscape of neoliberal pluralism and global capitalism that consumes difference as an alibi so that it does not make a difference.

Interestingly, the group that profits most from diversity politics and gender mainstreaming is white, bourgeois, and heterosexual.[6] Even

---

6   A good example of this "institutional farce" is the research group "Black Knowledges" at the University of Bremen that focuses on *New Black Diaspora Studies*, but is an exclusively white initiative without participation of Black scholars. Similarly women of color, migrants, and trans*persons are under-represented at Gender studies centers that disproportionately employ bourgeois, white, heterosexual scholars worldwide. In India, for instance, there is a growing nationwide pattern where dominant upper castes are increasingly demanding reservation benefits that were constitutionally allocated for marginalized and disenfranchised communities.

as critical race theory, postcolonial studies, diversity, intersectionality, migration, and globalization studies are increasingly core areas of feminist scholarship, the appropriation of knowledge of marginalized collectivities such as migrants and diasporic subjects in promoting the career of hegemonic groups is widespread. This prompts us to ask whether the highly celebrated discourses of diversity and intersectionality deliver equally to all constituencies or whether they function as an instrument for the differential distribution of rights and justice and as career making machines for intellectual elites. Interestingly, straight white men are increasingly staging themselves as victims of diversity politics, even as the pedagogical deployment of intersectionality in feminist scholarship results in re-securing the centrality of the subject positioning of white women (Puar, 2012, p. 52). Women of color, on the other hand, who were supposed to emerge as new subjects of feminism through intersectional analysis, are deployed as simply "articulating a grievance," even as the category is emptied of its specific meaning through scholarly overuse (ibid.).

Another crucial question that needs to be addressed in this context is the status of different categories that are legacies of the modernist imperial project. Being a corrective methodology, one can ideally hope from intersectionality research and diversity strategies to overcome the normative violence inherent in categories such as gender or sexuality even as they mitigate the overemphasis on one category at the cost of neglecting others. Against the straightforward understanding of intersectionality as the analysis of simultaneous inequalities, it would be more meaningful to examine why specific inequalities are given more importance than others in specific moments in specific spaces. Accordingly, the analyses should explore the entanglements of different factors or categories, even as it makes visible how "gender" and "race" or "class and "race" function as conflicting categories of analysis, whilst some categories appear to be more salient than others in specific contexts. For example, the focus on caste within the Indian context is more relevant than race[7] – and this is also pertinent for understanding the relations of power within the Indian diaspora. Similarly, categories such as *"First Nations," "Native Americans,"* or *"pueblos originarios"* cannot be simply subsumed under the umbrella term "race" and even less under that of "migration". Neglecting these nuances substantially distorts any examination of (historical) processes of discrimination. Similarly, an over-emphasis on "race" can lead to "class" being disregarded, as Gopal (2015) points out. Spivak explicitly cautions against solely focusing on race and (anti)-racism within the global North, as this does not automatically entail an engagement with the international division of labor, which she considers imperative (Spivak, 1990, p.126). She warns that such a narrow approach does not allow for a contestation of the complex strategies of economic, political, and social disenfranchisement within processes of decolonization:

> I was trying to show how our lives, even as we produce this chromatist discourse of anti-racism, are being constructed by that international division of labor, and its latest manifestations are in fact the responsibility of class-differentiated non-white people in the Third World, using the indigenous structures of patriarchy and the established structures of capitalism. To simply foreclose or ignore the international division of labor because that's complicit with our own production, in the interests of the black-white division as representing the problem, is a foreclosure of neo-colonialism operated by chromatist race-analysis. (Spivak, 1990, p. 126)

Along similar lines, postcolonial scholars caution that the focus on "race" as *the* prominent category within anti-colonial formations of resistance

---

7   With the increasing migration from different African countries to India and repeated racist attacks against African students, tourists, and businessmen and women, the importance of 'race' in analyzing discrimination is on the rise.

has meant that decolonization is equated with dismantling of racist structures and narratives. As Mahmood Mamdani rightly observes, the historical legitimacy of nationalist governments after decolonization was principally measured in terms of whether they initiated an effective de-racialization (Mamdani, 1996, p. 288). Mamdani reminds us that this resulted in "de-racialization without democratization," for instance, in Sub-Saharan Africa (ibid.). Framed as "indigenization program" or as "nationalization," one of the primary aims was to dismantle the privileges that white colonizers had accumulated through racist and imperialist politics. Along similar lines, postcolonial regimes are critiqued for not adequately addressing pre-colonial, colonial, and postcolonial heteronormativities.

In contrast, the debate surrounding intersectionality is at risk of fetishizing the race-class-gender mantra without paying attention to what issues are rendered invisible and excluded because of this mechanical repetition and Eurocentric reduction. It is no coincidence that the ritualized citation reminds one of the Christian holy trinity. Moreover, whenever the standardized list of categories is quoted, it either conceals other forms of oppression or freezes them into an "etcetera". In addition, Davina Cooper (2004) states that the problem of an intersectional perspective also lies in losing sight of the co-constitution of identities and inequalities, which do not result from intersectional categories. The demand that the intersecting categories be outlined in a clear and orderly manner that is quantifiable and verifiable stems from the fear of having to engage with nebulous and messy dynamics of political power. Irritation and disorientation that result from dealing with the complexities of social injustice are seemingly tamed through strict methodological guidelines. Ultimately one can observe a comeback of not only a universalist perspective but also of essentialist tendencies.

In *Gender Trouble* Judith Butler alludes to this when she mentions the almost embarrassing "etc." at the end of the "list of categories" (cf. Butler, 1990, p. 143). Here the "etcetera" as punctuation mark can simultaneously be interpreted as exhaustion and excess and should be the starting point for feminist self-critique. Once again universalist practices gain access through the backdoor by way of the dominant particular. This is why Butler clearly cautions against a politics that aims to create "positions" from where excluded groups can speak. Herewith she objects to a logic in which "positions" function as immaculate, coherent "categories" (Butler, 1993, pp. 111). In her view, the effort should not be to think race, sexuality, and gender in relation to each other *as if* they are "fully separable axes of power" (ibid., p.116). Rather, the theoretical proliferation of "categories" or "positions" should itself be questioned. Similar to Butler, Menon (2015) raises the question whether intersectional analysis should limit itself to analyzing marginalized and privileged positions or whether a more urgent and radical critical intervention necessitates a destabilization of the same.

Intersectionality versus Assemblage: The Politics of Positionality and Fluidity

An attempt to supplement intersectionality as a tool for political intervention is made by Jasbir Puar (2012), whose mobilization of the Deleuzean idea of assemblage[8] offers a mapping of fleeting, de-centered, and unstable bodies as opposed to politics of intersectional subject positioning. Puar explains that "intersectional identities are the byproducts of attempts to still and quell the perpetual motion of assemblages, to capture and reduce them, to harness their threatening mobility" (2012, p. 50). While intersectionality deploys the subject as a primary analytic frame and is concerned with multiplicity of subject identity, assemblage is marked by openness for the unknown

---

8   As Puar (2012, p. 57) explains, assemblage is not an assortment of things, nor is it a statement about states of affairs, rather it indicates practices, relations, connections, and patterning of energies, forces, and affects that give rise to concepts and content. It is more important to understand what assemblage *does* than what it *is*. Assemblage outlines the affective conditions necessary for the event-potential to unfold (ibid., p. 61).

and indeterminate. As opposed to the fixity of categories, identities, representations, and naming that informs the intersectional approach, the concept of assemblage addresses the messiness and contingency of forces and practices. Although intersectionality and assemblage both work towards examining how subjects emerge as effects of specific historical, economic, social, cultural, and political conditions, unlike Crenshaw Puar does not stop at addressing the co-constitution of racism, sexism, heterosexism, ablebodiedness, but concerns herself with biopolitics. Instead of analyzing difference in terms of race, class, gender, sexuality, religion, or even the category 'human,' the focus is on temporality, corporeality, and affect. In contrast to the intersectional attention to the political identity of women of colour, the Deleuzian notion of assemblage is about the fluid entanglements between disparate and multiple elements that are jumbled together without being neatly organized. There is no organic whole, but rather lines of articulation, segmentarity, strata, territories, flight, and movements of destratification and deterritorialization (ibid.). Assemblage is unattributable, namely, multiplicity without attributes that deprivileges positionality. Identities are considered to be multicausal, multidirectional, and liminal. Instead of bodies with identifiable gender, race, or other characteristics, the focus is on becoming, intensity, acceleration, rupture, and speed. Assemblage is marked by constant transformation, wherein properties of the constituent elements disappear and emerge in other forms. There are no underlying organizational principles, rather corporeality and embodiment is constituted through registers of consolidation.

In place of the intersectional focus on the additive power of discrimination or disenfranchisement, assemblage, through analysis of the capture of movement and controlling lines of flight, examines how stratified, hierarchical spaces and inequalities are created (ibid.). While the intersectional analysis ends up explaining identity in terms of a finite set of combinations of various recognized categories, assemblage identities are subversively unintelligible, thereby enabling interventions outside the normative frames. Empirical approaches understandably favor policy-friendly intersectionality to assemblage theory, for the former offer neat categories in which a combination of traits can help understand social phenomena, while the latter frustrate straightforward data collection and analysis. In response to the doubts about the political applicability of assemblage theory in contrast to the usefulness of intersectionality as a successful tool for social and scholarly transformation, Puar (2012, p. 50) upholds the efficacy of nonrepresentational, non-subject-oriented politics as proposed by Gilles Deleuze. Another important critique of intersectionality from the perspective of assemblage theory is its "problematic reinvestment in the humanist subject" (Puar, 2012, p. 55). This intervention questions whether "the marginalized subject is still a viable site from which to produce politics, much less whether the subject is a necessary precursor for politics" (ibid.) and whether new forms of exclusions are produced in the process of promoting inclusion through the determination of identity through discourses of difference. In "de-exceptionalizing" human subjectivities and bodies (Puar, 2012, p. 57), the performativity of politics is framed beyond human agency. Rather than understanding subjectivity in terms of embodied identities, categories like race, gender, sexuality become encounters, variations, and arrangements between bodies that emerge through processes of deterritorialization and reterritorialization (ibid.).

While Puar is critical of the narrowness of the representation politics of intersectionality and the identitarian interpellations it invokes, Kathy Davis argues that "intersectionality promises feminist scholars of all identities, theoretical perspectives, and political persuasions that they can "have their cake and eat it, too". (Davis, 2008, p. 72). In contrast to Davis, who emphasizes the strengths of intersectional approaches, we would like to draw further attention to some negative aspects that indicate an impossible desire for "one size fits all" diagnosis. Davis argues that intersectional approaches initiate a "discovery process," which not only promises new critical insights, but is ongoing and thus potentially never-ending (ibid.). However, in our view, the global North remains the key point of reference around which critique is formulated, and thus the perspective remains Eurocentric. Categories such as sexuality and class are marginalized, although they form important organizing principles for processes of decolonization. All in all, it can be said that the perfunctory repetition of the race/class/gender formula constitutes a problem of universalism and therefore one of depoliticization of critical interventions.

This raises the following questions: Who profits from intersectionality and diversity politics? Do they, for example, give subalternized subjects the opportunity to intervene in hegemonic structures or do they instead reify dominant academic discourses and political practices? Does this not end up with the global North once again being self-absorbed in the guise of justice?

Especially the coalescing of intersectionality and interdependence theories can be politically risky in that it neglects the transnational dimension of inequality and injustice. The interdependence approach refers to the reciprocal dependency of nation states, particularly with regard to their economic structures. The other question that needs to be addressed is whether the focus on identities is at the expense of neglecting structures. The aim here is not to revive the old debate between recognition versus redistribution or give priority to political economy over cultural practices. For it is obvious that reductionist economic analyses are just as problematic as "mere" cultural perspectives. No collective "only" suffers from economic exploitation just as no collective is "only" victim of cultural oppression. Furthermore recognition should not be understood as a goal in itself with no link to the question of redistribution. Our approach neither rejects intersectionality or diversity nor does it favor class politics over race, gender, or sexuality. Hierarchizing political fields would be counter-productive, even as stringent intellectual contemplation of the function of different categories within contemporary geopolitics is urgent. Here it is important to take Crenshaw's warning seriously when she advises that: "Intersectionality should not become a competition between those claiming oppression".[9] Spivak similarly remarks:

---

9   Kimberle Crenshaw at the conference "Celebrating Intersectionality?", Goethe University Frankfurt on 23.01.2009.

To see the problem of race simply in terms of skin color does not recognize that the only arena for that problem is the so-called white world, because you are focusing the problem in terms of blacks who want to enter and live in the white world, under racial laws in the white world. That obliges us to ignore the fact that in countries which are recognized as Third World countries, there is a great deal of oppression, class oppression, sex oppression, going on in terms of the collusion between comprador capitalists and that very white world. The international division of labor does not operate in terms of good whites, bad whites and blacks. A simple chromatism obliges you to be blind to this particular issue because once again it's present in excess. (Spivak, 1990, p. 126)

The critical impulses offered by intersectional approaches are politically important, as pointed out by even critics like Puar. This is why it is necessary to explore their limitations in order to revitalize them. In light of our entangled histories and futures, it is politically naïve to locate political responsibility within national boundaries. Despite various efforts to overcome the economic determinism and understand power and oppression from a multi-dimensional perspective, the intersectional approach and diversity politics fail precisely because they disregard transnational dimensions of social inequality as a legacy of colonialism. This leads us to the challenges of operationalizing intersectionality and diversity in the context of undoing injustice and inequality domestically as well as globally.

Righting wrongs

From a postcolonial perspective, the notions of gender justice and equality, which are key norms of intersectionality and diversity politics, are embedded within historical processes of righting past wrongs, even as they frame contemporary discourses of development politics and human rights (see Spivak, 2004). These norms determine what qualifies as unjust and what mechanisms and tools are considered adequate to undoing wrongs. They also determine who is heard and who has the power to refuse to listen (see Spivak, 1994/1988; also Castro Varela/ Dhawan, 2015, pp. 186).

Different understandings of the means for achieving gender justice and equality impose competing roles and expectations on national and international actors and organizations (ibid.). On the one hand, the state is increasingly being replaced by non-state actors like international NGOs and representatives of social movements, who enjoy a high level of legitimacy in the international public sphere to globally monitor issues of human rights abuses. On the other hand, it is argued that the state is indispensable for redistributive justice even as it should be held responsible for protecting its citizens. Varying interpretations of the role of governments, international organizations, and civil society actors produce very different strategies for gender justice such as empowerment of vulnerable persons through enabling political participation or economic self-sufficiency through provision of micro-credits or gender mainstreaming. Understanding the ideological and cultural legitimization for subordination of vulnerable groups within each arena can help identify how to overcome injustice.

An intersectional approach unfolds how justice in the realm of gender politics is not just a question of equality between the sexes; it also includes other factors like race, class, religion, and able-bodiedness, to name a few. This implies that women (or men) cannot be identified as a coherent or homogenous group. Instead, gender cuts across all social categories, producing different conceptions of justice. As pointed out by postcolonial scholars, processes of justice – economic, social as well as political – go hand in glove with processes of democratization and decolonization, which must be framed transnationally. In summary, the question of decolonization must neither be limited to anti-racist politics in the global North nor a celebration of diversity, plurality, and difference in the metropolis. Otherwise diversity politics ends up being a catchy "feel good" marketing strategy (as with "United Colors of Benetton"), which makes sure that differences don't make a difference. At the same time, stringent criticism and rigorous introspection will make transparent the blind-spots implicit in an intersectional approach against the backdrop of current structures of global interdependence and contemporary geopolitics. Nowadays it should be impossible to imagine a critical political practice that does not take the global dimensions of social inequality into account. Despite varied efforts to understand power and domination from a multi-dimensional perspective, the intersectional approach at times fails at meeting this challenge, because of its disregard of transnational dimensions that are a direct consequence of colonialism (Castro Varela, 2015, pp. 298). In our view the predominant focus on metropolitan spaces within academic debates on intersectionality and diversity can be read as symptomatic for an implicit Eurocentrism. In contrast to Menon's critique, which stresses the non-transferability of concepts and disregard of postcolonial contexts, we consider it problematic that the structural effects of international labor division and the overexploitation of third world gendered labor is inexcusably neglected within debates on intersectionality. In light of the focus on the global scope of justice, the political challenge we face, in our opinion, requires a rethinking of a methodological nationalism, which follows the "assumption that nation/state/society is the natural social and political form of the modern world" (Wimmer/Glick-Schiller, 2002, p. 302). The global North and the global South are interwoven within a context of economic interdependence, which is characterized by a power asymmetry and a history of imperialism. It is therefore urgent to problematize the production of dominant epistemologies and methodologies, which privilege the perspectives of the global North that are a consequence of neocolonial systems of power. At the same time, the everyday situation of vulnerable subjects within the global South, for example, the daily experiences of oppression and exploitation of *Dalit* women in India, as mentioned by Menon, are overlooked. It is imperative to apply a postcolonial historical perspective that takes macro-economic structures into account in order to understand and analyze how current dynamics of global interdependence have emerged and the challenges they bring with them. It neither suffices to list diverse grounds of discrimination without employing a historical as well as transnational perspective, nor is it helpful to uncritically conjure transnational alliances or to simply push for a subversion of social categories, in the hope that once we overcome differences, they will stop making a difference. This is the promise made by the free market as well as populist politics, namely, that we live in a post-feminist, post-racial world. As evidence we are offered examples of successful men and women, both black and white, as proof of effective diversity politics.

If colonialism was marked by economic exploitation, political domination, undermining of indigenous socio-political institutions, and deprecation of non-European epistemologies, neo-colonialism has ushered in economic and social restructuring globally. In light of this, the tools that have constituted the arsenal of postcolonial feminist scholarship need to be refashioned. Although feminist initiatives are increasingly transnational, the notion of "women's interest" shared by all regardless of race, class, religion, and nationality has led to advocating general solutions to global problems, which are seen to apply to all women universally. Gender programs for transnational justice often represent Third World women as "in need of help," thereby legitimizing external intervention. Insofar as Western feminists have participated in these kinds of universalizing political discourses and denied the possibility of non-Western forms of gender justice, they have contributed to reinforcing the Eurocentric bias in the pursuit of justice, whilst holding on to a form of solidarity that reinforces established hierarchies.

Spivak reproaches Western feminists like Martha Nussbaum for appropriating "Third World" women's narratives in order to find a "philosophical justification for universalism;" rather than being open to the other, Nussbaum brings "the other into the self" (Spivak, 2004, pp. 567-8). Emphasis on an ever-expanding catalogue of rights is dangerously confused with empowerment of third world women. The problem of the universalization of human rights is particularly visible in the domain of gender rights. The main issue here is that women's rights discourse essentializes "local culture". CEDAW, for example, takes Western rights as modern and per se emancipatory, while locating the source of "Third World" women's oppression mainly in the domain of traditional cultural practices, legitimizing the idea that modernity frees them. Violence against women is fetishized, reinforcing notions of barbaric and patriarchal African, Hindu, or Islamic traditions (Kapoor 2008, pp. 35).

The culturalization and individualization of women's rights diverts attention from broader questions of global structural inequality. While human/gender rights are being promoted by Western development organizations, many Western governments have a history of supporting brutal, authoritarian regimes in the global South. Moreover, it is important to note that many human/gender rights violations are the direct result of structural adjustment policies, promoted by some of the same donors that now dispense human rights (Kapoor 2008, pp. 36). States' flaunting of rights by banning unionization, disciplining women workers, supporting child labor, allowing lower-than-minimum wages, turning a blind eye to toxic working conditions, and cutting food and education subsidies are all legacies of neoliberal adjustment policies. Thus ironically even those development agencies, which are critical of structural adjustment, for instance human rights NGOs, end up reinforcing neo-colonialism when they uncritically promote liberal-universalist human rights (Castro Varela, 2011; Dhawan, 2014). The rights agenda serves to consolidate the institutional power of international organizations, while functioning as an alibi for strategic or military intervention, often under the pretense of "responsibility to protect" (Spivak, 2004).

The critique of what one cannot not want

In our opinion the future of anti-discrimination and global justice politics lies in an "affirmative sabotage" (Spivak, 2012), a strategy that transforms the instruments of the dominant discourse into tools for its transgression. Despite its implicit non-performativity, diversity and intersectionality politics remain indispensable: "we cannot not want them" (ibid, p. 4). Accordingly, instead of a categorical rejection of the ideologies of the rights-bearing subject, we plead for a reconfiguration and supplementation of norms that inform these approaches by inquiring into what is prior to and beyond what is recognized as legitimate political subjectivity. Furthermore, the deployment of a transnational perspective, which is historically informed, is imperative. We need to confront the paradox that whenever categories are listed with the aim of providing a comprehensive analysis of varied grounds of discrimination or exclusion, this itemization risks concealing certain moments of oppression that are not adequately reflected by these inventories. There is the danger of inadvertently homogenizing and essentializing messy social identities, experiences, and practices. What is urgently needed is a deconstructive vigilance with regard to both the categories as well as the frames of analysis. Political interventions need to be context specific even as they must overcome "methodological nationalism" to encompass both the local and the global. They should proffer strategies of resistance without disavowing that resistance produces its own registers of exclusion and appropriation. And finally, as Menon rightly points out: "The subject of feminist politics has to be brought into being by political practice". Here intersectionality and diversity can make an important contribution if conditions of non-performativity can be overcome.

References

Ahmed, S. (2006). The non-performativity of anti-racism. *Merideans: Journal of Women, Race and Culture, 7 (1)*, 104-126.

Anzaldúa, G. & Moraga, C. (1981). *This bridge called my back: Writings by radical women of color.* Gastonia, North Carolina: Persephone Press.

Butler, J. (1990). *Gender trouble: Feminism and the subversion of identity.* New York/London: Routledge.

Brown, W. (2015). *Undoing the demos. Neoliberalism's stealth revolution.* New York: Zone Books.

Combahee River Collective (1984[1978]). The Combahee River Collective Statement. In B. Smith (Ed.), *Home girls: A black feminist anthology* (pp. 264-274). New York: Kitchen Table: Women of Color Press.

Castro Varela, M. (2011). 'Wir haben das Recht auf kostenlose Geschirrspülmaschine'. Soziale Gerechtigkeit, Recht und Widerstand'. In María do Mar Castro Varela/ & N. Dhawan (Eds.). *Soziale (Un) Gerechtigkeit: Kritische Perspektive auf Diversität, Intersektionalität und Anti-Diskriminierung* (pp. 36-61). Münster: LIT.

Castro Varela, M. & Dhawan, N. (2015). *Postkoloniale Theorie: Eine kritische Einführung* (2nd ed.). Bielefeld: transcript.

Cooper, D. (2004). *Challenging diversity. Rethinking equality and the value of difference.* Cambridge: Cambridge University Press.

Crenshaw, K. (1991). Mapping the margins: intersectionality, identity politics, and violence against women of color. *Stanford Law Review, 43 (6),* 1241-1299.

Davis, K. (2008). Intersectionality as buzzword. *Feminist Theory, 19(1),* 67-85.

Dhawan, N. (2014). Affirmative sabotage of the master's Tools: The paradox of postcolonial enlightenment. In N. Dhawan (Ed.) *Decolonizing enlightenment: Transnational justice, human rights and democracy in a postcolonial world* (pp. 19-78). Opladen/Berlin/Toronto: Barbara Budrich.

Gopal, M. (2015). Struggles around gender: Some clarifications. *Economic & Political Weekly, 33,* 76-77.

Hall, S. (1989). Ethnicity: Identity and difference. *Radical America* 23, October/December, 9-20.

Hill Collins, P. (1990). *Black feminist thought: Knowledge, consciousness, and the politics of empowerment.* New York/London: Routledge.

John, M. E. (2015). Intersectionality. Rejection or critical dialogue? *Economic & Political Weekly, 33,* 72-76.

Kapoor, Ilan (2008). *The postcolonial politics of development.* New York. Routledge.

Lorde, A. (1984). *Sister outsider: Essays and speeches.* Portland, Oregon: The Crossing Press.

Mamdani, M. (1996). *Citizen and subject: Contemporary Africa and the legacy of late colonialism.* Princeton: Princeton UP.

Menon, N. (2015). Is Feminism about 'women'? A critical view on intersectionality from India. *International Viewpoint - online socialist magazine.* Retrieved from: www.internationalviewpoint.org/spip.php?article4038

Mohanty, C. T. (1984). Under western eyes: Feminist scholarship and colonial discourses. *Boundary, 2(12/3),* 333-358.

McClintock, A. (1995). *Imperial leather. Race, gender and sexuality in the colonial contest.* New York/London: Routledge.

Puar, J. K. (2012). I would rather be a cyborg than a goddess: Becoming-intersectional in assemblage theory. *Philosophia, 2(1),* 49-66.

Rich, A. (1986). *Blood, bread, and poetry: Selected prose, 1979-1985* (pp. 210-231). New York: Norton.

Spivak, G. C. (1994/1988). Can the subaltern speak? In P. Williams & L. Chrisman (Eds.), *Colonial discourse and post-colonial theory: A reader* (pp. 66-111). Hemel Hemstead: Harvester Wheatsheaf.

Spivak, G. C. (1990). *The post-colonial critic. Interviews, strategies, dialogues* (Ed. Sarah Harasym). New York/London: Routledge.

Spivak, G. C. (2004). Righting wrongs. *South Atlantic Quarterly 103(2-3),* 523-581.

Spivak, G. C. (2012). *An aesthetic education in the era of globalization.* Cambridge: Harvard University Press.

Suleri, S. (1995). Woman skin deep. Feminism and the postcolonial condition. In Ashcroft et al. (Eds.), *The post-colonial studies reader* (pp. 273-280). London/New York: Routledge.

Trinh, M. (1989). *Woman, native, other. Writing postcoloniality and feminism.* Bloomington/Indianapolis: Indiana University Press.

Wimmer, A. & Glick-Schiller, N. (2002). Methodological nationalism and beyond: Nation-state building, migration and the social sciences. *Global Networks, 2(4)*, 301-3.

THREE

PITFALLS OF DIVERSITY MANAGEMENT WITHIN THE ACADEMY

Mechthild Nagel

State University of New York – College at Cortland

Correspondence:
Mechthild Nagel, Philosophy and Center for Gender and Intercultural Studies, SUNY Cortland
Mecke.Nagel@cortland.edu

Abstract:

A brief historical overview of the ideological shift from multicultural education towards diversity education suggests that the "struggle" paradigm of the Civil Rights Movement has been abandoned in favor of celebrating differences. The paper discusses conflict-laden approaches of managing diverse voices, identities, and discourses within the U.S. academy.

Introduction

In North America, the urgency of integration, a key demand of a vibrant Civil Rights movement of the 1960s, gave rise to corporate concerns on how to manage a *multicultural* workforce. Since the

1980s, the multicultural appeal has lost its luster and corporations have increasingly focused on managing *diversity*. Diversity discourse left an indelible imprint on corporations and academe in the United States and elsewhere. Scholars took note of this political shift. James A. Banks, dubbed "the father of multicultural education," is a case in point. By 1981, he published a primer on *Cultural Diversity and Education* (now in its 6th edition, 2016), to adapt to the conservative turn in public policy. For instance, in the United States, inclusion strategies on narrowly defined multicultural (i.e. racial/ethnic) and gender grounds were considered inadequate (Nagel & Asumah, 2014). Demands for racial justice and women's rights were followed by a "lavender revolution" (i.e., LGBT human rights), and a struggle for recognition for people with disabilities. Black feminists articulated an intersectionality of social identities approach, to protest their endemic exclusion in white feminist and Black political thought. In this paper, I will show the conflict-laden, contentious approaches of managing diverse voices, identities, and discourses within a risk adverse, increasingly corporate academy. Calls for a paradigm shift in general education began with the new disciplines of Black Studies, Ethnic Studies, followed by Women's Studies. Importantly, these demands came from below, engendered by militant student protests, and were not a diversity management decision from above in the 1960s. These interdisciplinary studies programs were granted by besieged administrators (e.g., from San Francisco State, Cornell University, and the City University of New York) as a concession to a revolutionary student body that protested U.S. imperialist wars and racist state repression within its territory, especially on reservations and in cities (cf. Biondi, 2012). What are the lessons from the Civil Rights Movement for today's DREAMers,[1] Ban-the-Box activists, and for the Black Lives Matter social movement within U.S. academia, rallying for citizenship rights, for the rights of persons with conviction

---

1   Development, Relief, and Education for Alien Minors Act of 2013 grants conditional stay to young people without proper immigration papers. For a critique, see American Immigration Council (http://www. immigrationpolicy.org/issues/DREAM-Act).

records, and for racial equity within historically white institutions? Specifically, what did the struggles and educational practices that aimed at structural reforms look like from the vantage point of administrative report writers, namely those who are tasked with managing diversity?

To begin with, I argue that diversity management pivots around a subtle shift from a demand for *redistribution* to a fairly uncritical corporate frame of *recognition* of diversity (e.g. by addressing bias through sensitization workshops). Diversifying the academy seems to be an intrinsic good. Here I draw on Nancy Fraser's (1998) famous diremption, recognition vs. redistribution, but I do not support her own analysis and critique of recognition struggles from below. Rather, I draw on her critic's objection, i.e. that recognition and redistribution (in terms of reform or transformation) are always already intertwined concepts (Young, 1998). Iris Young holds that Fraser and other Left critics of multiculturalism overstate "the degree to which a politics of recognition retreats from economic struggles." To be sure, Young concedes that these "culture wars" have been the domain of university campuses (Young, 1998, p. 51). So, we want to ask: Does diversity management always lend itself to an accommodationist strategy, valuing recognition over economics? If so, what are its implications? I offer case studies, from the State University of New York (SUNY) and the City University of New York (CUNY), and I will address what diversity celebration looks like from the vantage point of those who are minoritized, as students who can't get access and as faculty and chief diversity officers who struggle along as they climb the ladder of mis/recognition.

The Demand of Access and Equity—The Dream of an Open University (Deferred)

The university has always been a bastion of privilege for the learned (and wealthy, male) elites. After 1945, the GI bill brought a great expansion of the landscape of public colleges and universities, including the establishment of the State University of New York (SUNY) system and the largest urban university system, the City University of New York

(CUNY). New York was the last state to establish a public university
(Clark *et al.*, 2010; Steck, 2012). Uniquely, a high school diploma
guaranteed many poor Jewish and non-Jewish white residents of New
York City access to the Free Academy or City College in Harlem.
Putatively, these were the best and brightest high school students,
however, dropout rates were very high (Traub, 1994). Residency was
a measure of positive discrimination as an antidote for *private* colleges
and universities which adopted other forms of discrimination, namely,
on the basis of race, creed, color or national ancestry, targeting Jewish,
Blacks, Italians (Berkowitz, 1948). Berkowitz's revealing report made
the case for a public university system on moral and political grounds,
prohibiting racist and anti-Semitic admission practices. His is perhaps
the first publication that assesses (and validates!) Black students'
attitudes regarding the importance of addressing a chilly campus climate
at historically white institutions of higher learning. The landmark
U.S. Supreme Court decision *Brown v. Board of Education* in 1954
determined that the chilly educational climate needed to be corrected
through systematic integration efforts. That decision created the moral
and legal basis for integrating Black and white schools throughout the
South (and the rest of the United States). The lofty goal of integration
was accepted by the white male justices with the proviso of "deliberate
speed." It meant that the implementation would proceed at a snails'
pace and such delays in turn created moral outrage and reasons for the
ensuing Civil Rights Movement.

New York state actors also were in no hurry implementing the state
university system in the 1950s. It was not until Nelson Rockefeller's
election as governor that the vision of a massive university system
(SUNY) was fully implemented. Governor Rockefeller has also been
credited with skillfully maneuvering around the interests of private
colleges and universities, upstate constituents, and civil rights activists
(Shermer, 2015). The opening of junior colleges, medical and law
schools, and Catholic colleges towards the "giddy multitude" (cf. Takaki,
1993) brought along demands for an inclusive curriculum to reflect the
lived experience of students and an increasingly diverse professoriate.

Multicultural education began to shape many general education programs and created further demands for a radical transformation of the university, including diversifying its monocultural professoriate. Open and free access for students of color was one such radical goal, won by Black and Puerto Rican students in the famous 1969 Open Admissions Strike at CUNY. They also demanded that education majors take mandatory courses in Black and Puerto Rican history as well as Spanish. In an unprecedented way, the CUNY students not only pushed back the threat of Rockefeller's budget cuts but instead brought about the doubling of the student body of CUNY. Administrators felt under siege and acted fast in order to gain control. Thanks to the continued militancy by the next generation of students, the open admissions policy lasted for three decades, thus transforming an elite white university system into a racially diverse and working class one in an unparalleled way. However, the free tuition policy lasted only some five years (*CUNY Matters*, 2011; CUNY History, n.d.; Traub, 1994).

Rockefeller, the son of the elite, kept pushing for tuition for CUNY schools but his plans only succeeded after he resigned as governor. While in office, Rockefeller was not only known for his stewardship for a premier public higher education system, but he was also responsible for ordering the mass shooting of prisoners to end the Attica rebellion in 1971. Soon thereafter, he established the most repressive drug laws in the nation, a formula for "crime control" which was spearheaded by U.S. president Nixon, who ordered a "war on drugs" to decimate Black Power politics and to repress the Black-led Civil Rights movement (Hanson, 2016; Perez & Saldaña, 2016). The Rockefeller Drug Laws spurred an unprecedented built up of prisons in upstate New York, and it targeted fairly exclusively downstate Black and Latino non-violent youth for life-long prison sentences. Dollar for dollar state funding shifted from investment in capital expenditures for SUNY (and CUNY) towards excessive prisons expenditures (Nagel, 2008). Not a single new college campus was built during the last thirty years.

The majority of Black and Latino folks live in segregated neighborhoods with substandard housing, public schools, inadequate access to good jobs, quality health care, supermarkets, recreational resources, etc. However, the state does not spare taxpayers' money for military hardware for policing, containing, and simply harassing residents of color, such that policy makers and activists now speak of a cradle-to-prison pipeline. Policy makers have noticed that when a child fails third grade, a prison cell will have to be budgeted, due to the likelihood of going to jail rather than finishing high school. Race, class, and geography all play a role whether one gets send to (drug) treatment or to prison (Mauer, 2006). The ascendancy of Barack Obama to the White House has not meant social or economic uplift for Black working class America (Alexander, 2010; Drucker, 2010; Porter, 2016; Rothwell, 2016). In *Savage Inequalities*, Jonathan Kozol (1991) already decried the caste system of schooling and found that segregation was worse in 1991 than in 1954, when the Supreme Court desegregated separate and unequal schools. Alexander's bestseller *The New Jim Crow* (2010) confirms Kozol's bleak assessment and brought to light the racial caste system vis-à-vis the treatment of Black men in the criminal justice system. The Nixon presidency, and Rockefeller, started the punitive politics of incarceration (mandatory minimum sentences, ending good time, ending furloughs, etc.) which gave rise to the myth of the criminalblackman (Russell-Brown, 2008) and neoliberal policies that dismantled social welfare infrastructure. These in turn contributed to massive increases in health care costs and, of course, in tuition, even for public colleges and universities, where a commitment to grant funding and other subsidies of economically disadvantaged and academically underprepared students has been shrinking. The racist effects present a double containment of Black working class people with the expansion of the prison system and with the legal and de facto attack on race-based affirmative action programs. Thanks to the Black Lives Matter movement, we may see some crumbling of structural impediments, but backlash is viscerally felt with the ascent of the Tea Party, the "Trump factor," and a religious belief in austerity, as public investments in the penal and military industrial complexes continue unabated.

The Reagan presidency brought an attack on affirmative action policies, buttressed by U.S. Supreme Court decisions which ruled against racial "quotas" (*Bakke* rule, 1978). President Kennedy had initiated affirmative action as a political appeasement strategy by offering affirmative action to those who were harmed by Jim Crow (segregationist) practices in the South and by racist discrimination elsewhere. It was meant as an empowerment strategy to give Black citizens opportunities for employment, advancement, and education. However, in practice the pool for eligible affirmative action groups was soon widened and businesses and colleges started to hire white women instead. Today, the biggest group of beneficiaries are veterans of war. Starting with president Reagan's ridicule of disadvantaged groups as "special interests" or racially charged slogans of ending welfare because of (Black) welfare queens abusing the system (sic), we have witnessed an erosion and subsequent cooptation of the Civil Rights Movement's "borning struggle;" this term was coined by Bernice Johnson Reagon (cf. Cluster 1979) to suggest that Black activists gave birth to a struggle for redistribution and recognition for all other social justice groups (American Indian Movement, second wave feminism, La Raza, the Stonewall uprising by trans, gay, and gender nonconforming Black people, etc.). Even though affirmative action program officers still have a place at the table of human resource offices in the U. S. university, their portfolios focus increasingly on risk management and mandatory sexual harassment trainings, as well as offering resources on how to increase a diverse pool of applicants. There are no sanctions for recalcitrant departments which repeatedly resort to hiring cis men who are straight, white, and able-bodied and have not been trained in decolonizing their disciplines.

The Reagan administration also ushered in a backlash against multicultural education, which conservative think tanks such as the Heritage Foundation furthered with headlines about the dangers of multiculturalism and shored up with Islamophobic sentiments after Samuel Huntington's publication of "The Clash of Civilizations?" (1993). Most recently conservative journalists use a shrill defense of cultural assimilation (i.e., Euro-American, Christian values) targeting refugees, preferably those who practice Islam, and their left-wing apologists in the academy and encouraging European governments to take note of the peril of non-occidental values and peoples (Gonzalez, 2016). Such a conservative turn is a particularly troubling tendency in primary education, because teachers are often captive to the ideological leanings of school boards and to monocultural standards by federal and state education departments, which schools of education within universities have to adopt in order to get accreditation. Liberal educators such as Banks (2016) also admonish that competent multicultural educators should not "make students cynics nor ... encourage them to desecrate European heroes such as Columbus and Cortés" (p. 11). By contrast, progressive authors such as Howard Zinn, *A People's History of the United States* (1980), Angela Y. Davis, *Women, Race, and Class (1981)*, Bill Bigelow and Bob Peterson, *Rethinking Columbus* (2003) or James Loewen, *Lies My Teacher Told Me* (1995), Jonathan Kozol, *Savage Inequalities* (1991) go "astray" and offer a cogent ideology critique of triumphalist U.S. history telling. Their counternarratives to crass patriotism provide histories from below which resonate with diverse student populations, whereas standardized, white-washed victors' histories may hinder quality education and produce oppressive outcomes. In fact, a Mexican-American studies curriculum in a school district in Arizona was shut down because it defied parroting the patriotic racial frame so prevalent in schools across the United States. Might it be dangerous recognition politics that a Chicana student should find herself reflected in the stories told about conquest, genocide, and persistent struggles against racism? Indeed. A school commission report showed that teaching progressive revisionist history to Chicanos and Chicana children enhances critical thinking skills and increases students' academic performance. White politicians filed a lawsuit and denounced ethnic studies for creating resentment against whites. A judge agreed. Instead of pursuing the commission's recommendation of expanding a Mexican American Studies program, it was shut down (*Huffington Post*, 2013). Here are the markings of the ultimate cooptation of Affirmative Action cum multicultural politics of recognition: whites are now the veritable victims of history told from the vantage point of people of color.

In this politically charged climate and a veritable corporate intrusion into education and standards, e.g. by the British-based Pearson Corporation (Reingold, 2015), the mainstream curriculum that touches on diversity education is filled with feel-good, colorblind rhetoric; the teacher's focus is on prejudice reduction (cf. Banks, 2016) and not raising questions about systemic inequality and divide-and-conquer victor's history (e.g., settler colonialism, capitalism, chattel slavery). Recently, Texas schoolbooks eliminated the word "slave" in favor of "workers" who were transported from Africa, till a Black parent protested and created a social media outburst of resistance (Moser, 2015). More euphemisms endorsed by the Texas Board of Education include the following: "The slave trade would be renamed the 'Atlantic triangular trade,' American 'imperialism' changed to 'expansionism,' and all references to 'capitalism' have been replaced with 'free enterprise'" (Paulson, 2010).

Contradictions prevail in today's diversity landscape. The online newsletter *Insight Into Diversity* (May 2016) reports in the same issue, divergent trends: an increased focus on diversity and inclusion classroom strategies within Pomona College for tenure review, while in Tennessee, the legislature abolishes the diversity office at the University of Tennessee and redirects its funding to scholarships for minority engineering students. The reason: "State lawmakers had been threatening to withhold funding from the office since last year, after staff posted a guide for using gender-neutral pronouns and promoted inclusive ways to celebrate holidays, which angered some Republican lawmakers" (Prinster, 2016). Trans* struggles have risen in importance and even got unusual support: New York's governor Cuomo has issued a boycott for non-essential state travels to North Carolina. The Southern state has come under fire for its repressive (binary) bathroom politics, nullifying the right of transgender persons to use the bathroom that matches their gender identity (Governor Cuomo, Executive Order 155, 2016).

"The Fire Next Time"

We'll have to keep in mind that representation and redistribution struggles came from the streets and radicalized students took the fight into academia. They included armed takeovers, e.g., at Ivy League Cornell University in 1969 (Wilhelm, 2016) by black undergraduate students who were tired of the hegemonic Eurocentric curriculum. They demanded representation of diverse faculty whom they could confide in as mentors and teachers, who have the (cultural) competence to understand their frustrations and develop cognitive and psychosocial strategies for survival in a historically white institution. (The survival struggles of ALANAA faculty, i.e. African, Latina(o), Asian, Native and Arab Americans, will be discussed below.) Today's Black Lives Matter (BLM) social movement has repeated yester-years demands of radicalized students during the Civil Rights Struggle and the anti-Vietnam war activism. BLM started in 2012 with a nation-wide protest about the acquittal of George Zimmerman, a self-appointed vigilante cop who killed African American teenager Trayvon Martin in Florida. The protest action became a national movement in the aftermath of the police killing of another Black teenager Michael Brown in Missouri, 2014. In 2015, Black activists around the country took the fight into the academy to protest racism in the classroom, residential life, sports, and at the level of administrative leadership. In fact, these demands appear to be cyclical although the methods are vastly dissimilar thanks to the global reach of social media coupled with an intensification of government surveillance.

The government's ability to scrutinize student protesters today is unparalleled with respect to COINTELPRO, the FBI's secret counter intelligence program to spy on a multitude of social/political dissenters and to destroy the Black Panther Party. To date (December 2015), Black Lives Matter has spread to dozens of campuses and its non-violent actions have led to the resignation of several white senior administrators across the country (Wilson, 2015). It remains to be seen how their demands will be absorbed at historically white academic institutions. Thanks to the vibrant Black Liberation Collective, which encompasses Black Student Unions from over 80 universities, radical terminology and demands for redistribution of resources are back in vogue. They include resisting oppression, disrupting white hegemonic institutional power and consciously noting the interconnectedness of oppressive systems (racism, heterosexism, transphobia, class oppression, xenophobia, etc.). Their manifesto (BLC 2015) resonates with that of the Combahee River Collective (1977), a Black feminist statement that disrupted the monoculturalism of the second wave of white feminism in the 1970s. However, the CRC's insurgency demands remain an elusive ideal and instead their struggle paradigm was coopted and reframed into a diversity-cum-intersectionality model, which suggests that all social identities have equal value (Wallis, 2015). Will the Black Liberation Collective continue to disrupt the neoliberal ideological hegemony of the academy by demanding no tuition fees for Black and Indigenous peoples and the corporation's divestment from prison shares (Gladney, 2015)? Will the BLC continue to contest administrators who are happy to make concessions to symbolic recognition politics but divert attention away from debt-free demands and monetary reparations to descendants of enslaved persons on university grounds in the North as well as the South? Robin Kelley (2016) is hopeful:

> That the fire this time spread from the town to the campus is consistent with historical patterns. The campus revolts of the 1960s, for example, *followed* the Harlem and Watts rebellions, the freedom movement in the South, and the rise of militant organizations in the cities. But the size, speed, intensity, and character of recent student uprisings caught much of the country off guard. Protests against campus racism and the ethics of universities' financial entanglements erupted on nearly ninety campuses, including Brandeis, Yale, Princeton, Brown, Harvard, Claremont McKenna, Smith, Amherst, UCLA, Oberlin, Tufts, and the University of North Carolina, both Chapel Hill and Greensboro.

> These demonstrations were led largely by black students, as well as coalitions made up of students of color, queer folks, undocumented immigrants, and allied whites.

Perhaps CUNY administrators were also caught off guard in 1969, when several African American and Puerto Rican students demanded desegregation. But they had to act quickly, since the students occupied buildings and even set one on fire. In the end, they ceded with a compromise to organized labor: open admissions for all city high school graduates. A report's subheading reads "policy by riot" (Renfro *et al.*, 1999, p. 19) and notes with disdain that CUNY sacrificed high standards ("excellence") for mere "access" when dispensing with standardized testing and offering remedial education for all underprepared first-year students: "Access and excellence are CUNY's historic goals. Over the past 30 years, the 'access' portion of the mission has overwhelmed the university at the expense of excellence" (Renfro *et al.*, 1999, p. 1), a sentiment which James Traub's (1994) book on the City College put in motion with his critique of open admissions, i.e. affirmative action. Only recently, "inclusive excellence" has been used to overcome the opposites of "access" and "academic excellence," and politicians from Obama to education department officials extol the virtues of a diverse classroom as enriching the college experience for all. Yet, the Renfro report also reluctantly acknowledges that the senior colleges of CUNY have not kept their promise of access to Black and Latino students, thanks, of course, to the prohibition of race-based affirmative action measures. The recent U.S. Supreme Court decision on affirmative action (*Fisher II*, June 2016), reversing over thirty years of outlawing "quotas" and racial diversification of college admissions, breathes new life into "inclusive excellence." Interestingly, because of a shrinking pool of high school graduates admissions officers of SUNY are now forced to recruit in multicultural schools that they have in the past ignored. For decades, SUNY Cortland mainly recruited students from white dominated areas of Long Island and neglected racially diverse metropolitan areas such as Syracuse or New York City. Today, the incoming first-year cohort is about twenty percent students of color. However, the goal of inclusive excellence rings hollow, when only twenty-five percent of Black students graduate from the college, while whites graduate at the rate of seventy-two percent.

The Legal Context: The Meaning of Affirmative Action in an Age of Diversity Management

In 1961, during the militant "borning struggle" of the Black-led Civil Rights Movement, President Kennedy issued an executive order (10925) to prohibit racist discrimination in the workplace and also to encourage business to consider "affirmative action and equal opportunity" and diversifying their workforce (DiTomaso, 2013, p. 257). In his famous "I have a dream …" speech, Martin Luther King (1963) powerfully noted that Black people are still not free and furthermore, they have been given a bad check, which reads "insufficient funds." Kennedy had made a timid reparative gesture to Black America: apply to jobs and colleges, and some of you might get coveted college entry into historically white (and some elite) academic institutions, which were denied to generations of Black Americans due to Jim Crow practices of exclusion. It was a fantastical proposition: to attain placements despite cumulative disadvantages in education and second-class citizenship status.

The dream was deferred: In the end, the Executive Order concerning "Affirmative Action" was amended to address sex discrimination in the Johnson administration (DiTomaso, 2013, p. 257). As such, it turned out to be a corrective measure benefiting white middle class women (like myself) to get jobs that were beyond our dreams and reach in the 1960s. An elastic interpretation of "Affirmative Action" would include opening doors to white women, who were thought to "fit" into a white male boardroom with much greater ease than Black people and other folks of color. To date, what is left of Kennedy's lofty ideal is a mere nod to "equal opportunity." Or: everybody is affirmed, because we are all diverse!

Favoring a focus on "diverse voices" is akin to moving chairs around so that some workers of color will have front row seats (and being given prizes for their diversity work), but few, if any, new chairs will be added to the white dominated workplace, offering a cohort of people of color a seat at the table. Such liberal focus on awareness raising about inequalities has also left its imprint in the academy. Diversity trainers inform us about a plethora of social identities, which all (ought to) take up equal space: racism should be dealt with on a continuum of challenges such as classism (sic), ableism and sizeism/weightism/lookism (Wallis, 2015). And Audre Lorde (1983) is (mistakenly, I believe) quoted for her bon mot: "There is no hierarchy of oppressions."

So, it is interesting to see that today, military veterans are the single largest beneficiary group of scholastic opportunities and government employment, and many of them are white men. At all colleges and universities, another trend is noticeable: Many of the Black students enrolled (and a number of faculty/staff) are first (or second) generation immigrants.[2] It is easy to blame the victim, as politicians are quick to do. However, the deeper root of the problem, namely, a prison epidemic that

---

2　"[S]triking immigrant-generational status differences were found in analyses of the 1999 National Longitudinal Survey of Freshmen (NLSF; Charles et al., 2008; Massey *et al.*, 2007), which included more than 1,000 Black entering-freshmen at 28 selective colleges and universities. In 1999, Black immigrant-origin (i.e., first- or second-generation immigrant) entering freshmen made up 27% of the NLSF Black freshmen population, although they comprised only 13% of the U.S. Black population aged 18 to 19 (Massey *et al.*, 2007); they were thus over-represented by more than double their share in the population. Moreover, the proportion of immigrant-origin Black undergraduates increased as school selectivity increased: first- and second-generation Black immigrants made up 24% of Black students at the least selective institutions, but 41% at Ivy League schools. In fact, Charles and colleagues (2008) found that, even after controlling for students' social origins, academic backgrounds, and pre-collegiate experiences, second-generation African and Caribbean Black students were twice as likely as U.S.-origin (i.e., third-plus-generation) Black students to attend the most elite NLSF institutions" (Tauriac & Liem, 2012).

has ensnared practically every U.S. Black family: one in three Black men will face incarceration in his lifetime. In an era of mass incarceration, there are more Black males in prison than enrolled in colleges and universities. This has a lasting psychic impact. Testing has shown that Black male applicants *without* criminal records have a higher chance of being denied a job than *convicted* white males (with parole status, etc.). As Devah Pager writes: "The effect of race was very large, equal to or greater than the effect of a criminal record. Only 14 percent of black men without criminal records were called back, a proportion equal to or less than even the number of whites *with* a criminal background" (Pager, 2004, p. 46). President Kennedy did not sign a true reparative measure that included "guarantees" of jobs and education (never mind housing or excellent k-12 schooling). It was simply "an opportunity." So, in the post-Jim Crow era, people of color may be handed a job application, but it is not assured that they will get a call back, even when they are more qualified than white counterparts. And because of criminal records which are public information, admissions officers are prone to deny worthy applicants a place at the (college) table. The risk-averse academy gives no second chances thus ensuring that a "record" will follow the person for the rest of his or her life hampering significant educational opportunities and gainful employment (CCA, 2015).

Why is all this relevant for an analysis of diversity management? While all white institutions clamor for gifted U.S. born Black applicants, they also quietly pursue an internationalizing strategy, as their data of Black students (or faculty/staff) tend not to separate out national origin status, and the presence of African or Caribbean faculty and students will be all that matters to make the university look diverse. It is a matter of presenting a score sheet that receives a "diversity" stamp of approval by national organizations such as the National Association of Diversity Officers in Higher Education, *DiversityInc*, and regional educational accrediting agencies.

Diversity Tactics: Roles of Chief Diversity Officers in the Neoliberal University

Diversity Management is a *corporate* approach that, for the most part, ignores the complexities of lived experiences, of intersectional oppression, and lacks praxeological clarity: understanding the interaction of critical discourses and practices. As mentioned above with respect to the exclusion of applicants with convict status, it is a *risk-averse* approach, and it is peculiar how effortlessly diversity management has been introduced into the academic institutional framework. Students of color, still labeled by administrators as "minorities" (sic), disappear into aggregate statistics about recruitment, retention, and graduation rates. The term "diversity" lends itself to much confusion, being a hot topic among academics who engage with the term in a critical way, while administrators use it normatively or instrumentally (Vertovec, 2014, p.1).

In the SUNY system, which encompasses over 60 campuses including my own college, the Chancellor has pursued an ambitious diversity strategic plan promising to become "the most inclusive university system in the United States" (Zimpher, 2015, p. 3), She mandated every campus to appoint a Chief Diversity Officer to coordinate diversity management of all units and departments (Zimpher, 2015). So far, so good. In reality, these officers have this (impossible) mandate:

a) to conduct trainings of search committees in order to diversify the workforce while being one of a few diverse persons among the senior administration (reality of tokenism);

b) to assuage any conflicts rising from the student body (the most likely body that speaks up or worse, occupies the presidential suite) by inviting select students to join a diversity council.

c) to issue reports on diversity scores (aligning with national standards and practices);

d) to be the "fall person" in case something goes awry (the next racist incident, sexual assaults against women in fraternity housing, etc.); it will be the diversity officer who will take the blame, thus preventing a holistic review of systemic failures of providing a welcoming and safe environment for all;

e) to lead positive directives (award ceremonies given to those who have an equally positive outlook on diversity management).

f) to partner with faculty on curriculum initiatives (cf. Worthington *et al.*, 2014)

For any person considering advancing to the level of Chief Diversity Officer, it will be prudent to study some historical cases. For those of us who are employed by the State University of New York system (SUNY), it is paramount watching the Gallagher's documentary film *Brothers of the Black List* (2013), which chronicles the aftermath of the SUNY Oneonta administration's fateful decision of turning over a list of 125 Black male students to the city of Oneonta's police department in search of a suspect. This blatant incident of egregious racial profiling occurred a mere 20 years ago and the litigation was one of the longest civil rights suits in U.S. history. The film shows that the Multicultural Resource Director failed to be a resource for traumatized students; instead they turned to a Black college counselor for crisis intervention and advocacy.

Despite best intentions, the diversity officer's key role, in this hyperreal world of diversity management, is to shield the president and other power brokers from liability and to provide maximum damage control. Because they are "management confidential" or otherwise worry about job retention, these diversity officers are unlikely to go to bat for a Black student applicant with a criminal record and draw the ire of a powerful admissions director. If they are savvy, they call on allied faculty (with tenure) diversity workers to do the job they (as diversity officers) were hired for: assist in diversifying the student body, participate in "difficult dialogues" with admission officer, etc.

In fact, the diversity management blueprint for universities authorized by the National Association of Diversity Officers in Higher Education outlines the following social identity categories: race/ethnicity, gender, age, sexual orientation, disability, religion, national & geographic origin, language use, socio-economic status, first generation, veteran/ military, political ideology (Worthington *et al.*, 2014). So, in addition to protected classes of groups, one's worldview (including pagan or atheist) is also a notable diversity dimension. This blueprint is mentioned in SUNY Chancellor Zimpher's policy memorandum (September 2015).

What is notably still missing in the extensive list is "convict status." Worthington's policy paper that outlines national "Standards of Professional Practice for Chief Diversity Officers" leaves out a diverse group of people who exited the penitentiary to seek entry in the other place of higher learning. The effect of such a silence or benign neglect in this age of mass incarceration is that millions of U.S. citizens are quite intentionally locked out. By contrast, the other major public university system in New York state, namely CUNY—the City University of New York—consciously invites returning citizens to apply, because they do not have to check a box disclosing a felony conviction when they apply to CUNY schools. There is a silver lining. Thanks to the social activism by multi-racial coalitions and celebrity authors such as Michelle Alexander, whose book *The New Jim Crow* (2010) critiques a decades-old racist drug policy, the Obama Administration has rallied some two dozen universities and colleges together, including SUNY, to take a pledge to ban the box for student applicants with prior convictions (The White House, 2016). Perhaps thousands of New Yorkers will now get a second chance instead of permanent second-class citizenship.

Diversity Discourses – Civility Discourses ("we all need to get along")

So far, I have argued that the gains of the Civil Rights Movement have been slowly eroded. Discursively speaking, this means the virtual disappearance of critiques of power, hegemony, oppression, and ideology, and of course, resistance to systemic injustice (cf. Bart, 2016). Cultural critic Robin Kelley (2016) implores student activists to keep pushing the institutions into a life-affirming direction. He notes "resistance is our healing. Through collective struggle, we alter our circumstances; contain, escape, or possibly eviscerate the source of trauma; recover our bodies; reclaim and redeem our dead; and make ourselves whole. It is difficult to see this in a world where words such as *trauma, PTSD, micro-aggression,* and *triggers* have virtually replaced *oppression, repression,* and *subjugation*" (his emphasis). What was formerly discussed as problems of structural or systemic injustice is now being reduced to personal slights or personal responsibility, replete with counseling sessions and risk-management assessment reports.

During the academic year 2015-16, one campus performs diversity management in the following manner: The Black Student Union held town hall meetings on behalf of the Chief Diversity Officer and the campus administration. The president of BSU read out managerial language ostensibly to make such meetings safe for senior administrators and white students. Ground rules for engagement even suggested refraining from labeling one's traumatic experience as "racist." Instead, the speaker was encouraged to speak of it as "racialized experience" and do so within one minute of allowed airtime. Audience responses were collected and perhaps discussed at a President's Cabinet meeting. A faculty/staff committee on campus climate never received the responses and failed to make recommendations for a campus that values inclusive excellence. Perhaps these campus conversations offer up the hope that discussions about racism can be carried out in a "safe space" and welcome interracial dialogue. Yet, social media with anonymously posted hate mail or classroom discussions which pit students of color against the white teacher, who educates the class about race as a biological fact speak volumes of the presence of a racist climate, not a "racialized" one. Social media may be new, however, what is not new are the students of color complaints.

At SUNY Cortland, a report "Toward a more equitable, inclusive, and diverse academic community" (Steck *et al.*, 1992) makes clear that students of color should not be unfairly tasked with "instant expertise" on matters of urban affairs in a classroom, something that continues to haunt well-meaning white teachers' pedagogy today, as students' feedback makes clear. The Steck report also emphasizes the role of meaningful mentoring and recommends the expansion of a mentoring program for students of color. Twenty years later, this program that helped to retain students on campus was disbanded by an administrator, because it did not include white students. However, all strategic proposals regarding overcoming achievement gaps between white and student of color cohorts emphasize the role of advising and mentoring as a key to retention and graduating students of color within six years. Diversity management "levels the playing field" in a way that this tactic again disadvantages ethnically and racially diverse students on a white dominated campus. A subsequent report, "Recruitment and Retention of Ethnic Minority Report" (Peagler, 2000), focuses on key offices, including admissions and recommends: "The College should establish an on-going assessment of what is being accomplished related to campus climate and issues pertinent to diversity" (p. 14). However such committee has never put together an annual progress report (card), nor has it been tasked to report to the president of the college, as the Peagler report had advised.

Part and parcel of a risk-adverse strategy is to champion a "crucial conversations" re-education campaign. The ideological framework is focused on the *individual* (disgruntled) employee, who will need a "stern, but kind talk" with her supervisor. "Crucial conversations" packaged workshops were first tried out in the corporate world and then imported via Human Resources and Affirmative Action Officers to the academic context. This "effective communication" program whisks away any need for "diversity dialogues," e.g. regarding intent and impact of speech; it steers clear from any critical discussion of systemic powerlessness and a cycle of oppression. We are all supposed to belong (and behave civilly). And (ideally) employees would be "allowed" to talk back at their unkind boss, as long as they follow the civilly outlined rules of conduct. Supposedly, the workers do not have to fear retaliation. But noting a pattern of sexism or racism in the manager's actions would be anathema to the corporatist agenda of "crucial conversations" conduct: those are construed as fighting words and the complainant might face reprimand.

Diversity management often devolves into "managing" diversity: a homogenous, white (male) management presides over a workforce that may have a few white gays or lesbians or straight-identified persons of color in decision-making roles, but otherwise it relegates gender queer or gender fluid persons as well as ethnically and culturally diverse cis gender workers to the backroom, low-paying, and invisible, glass-ceiling and sticky-floors jobs such as janitorial staff (cf. Cox, 1991).

Hence, despite the ideal-case scenarios played in workshops and attention to socio-economic class (in theory), few workers, especially secretaries or professional salaried staff members dare to challenge a supervisor by challenging her to a "crucial conversation." Working class college professors with working class roots and first generation identity, because their parents never attended college, are also unlikely to speak up, even in contentious department meetings, lacking the required cultural capital and self-esteem (Kadi, 1996).

Within the U.S., this management model thrives on a post-Civil Rights business ideology of nominal inclusion of diverse populations and interest groups in the workforce and academic institutions. The model's focus is squarely on diversity trainings that minimize conflicts (e.g. "10 things not/never to tell your (diverse) co-worker," *DiversityInc*, n.d.). In the academic context, the awareness-raising approach is adopted by professionals who manage student affairs. Studies of private business companies show that training programs that simply target managerial bias are fairly ineffective, whereas "affirmative action plans, diversity committees, and diversity staff positions are more effective in increasing [workforce] diversity" (Wrench, 2014, p. 259). The business case for outcomes, i.e. diversifying the workforce, is indeed helpful and addresses the findings of perception research, identified by Sara Ahmed (2012):

> One project finds that external communities perceive the university as being white. Rather than responding by accepting this perception (and thus assuming the task of modifying the thing perceived as white) the perception becomes the problem. The task becomes changing the perception of whiteness rather than changing the whiteness of the organization. (p. 184)

This means that diversity managers draw the wrong conclusion by including more students of color in glossy welcoming brochures and promotion pictures in the admissions office. But the pictures of white professors adorning the hallways or offices of most departments cannot be changed, can they? However, one change might be, following Ahmed's analysis, that the smiling photographs of the white professoriate disappear from the walls. By contrast, effecting transformative change and making a "business" case for diversification, cluster hires of faculty of color have been quite effective in increasing their retention rates.

Yet, businesses also report a rise of conflicts in a diverse workforce and question the efficacy of conflict management. Do they simply reinforce double standards and double binds or do they dismantle structural, cultural, psychological barriers, and systemic exclusion?

Facing the Double Bind

The shared realities faced by ALANAA faculty in historically white institutions, can be summarized as "Sisyphean." Stephanie A. Fryberg and Ernesto J. Martínez's book (2014) shines a critical light on the presentation of data with respect to hiring and retention practices of faculty of color. "What does it mean for universities to claim progress with respect to diversifying faculty ranks when 73 percent of faculty of color hold non-tenure-track or adjunct faculty positions that do not provide job security (American Federation of Teachers, 2010)?" (2014, p. 5). Such claims of progress in diversifying the faculty hides in plain sight the fact that a myopic perspective is more comforting to gatekeepers at historically white institutions than an honest look at the macroscopic picture of understanding the diverse pressures faculty of color face vis-à-vis tenure-track level positions, especially at elite colleges or research universities.

In the case of tenure-track faculty of color, Fryberg and Martínez describe the presence of interrelated narratives that have all the trappings of a double-bind oppression, outlined in Marilyn Frye's (1983) classic article on oppression. What is considered meritorious research tends to be contested ("Striving, but Falling Short"), even as some scholars are applauded for tackling diversity or ethnography ("Inching toward Progress"), and their clincher: "Service Is (Not) Necessary." Several Ivy League institutions have been under scrutiny for failing to tenure its faculty of color and Black Lives Matter gives new attention to these interrelated oppressive narratives. Take the recent case of Professor Aimee Bahng who was denied tenure at Dartmouth College. An angry student post reads: "Professors who engage with activism & advocate for students are disproportionately denied tenure #Fight4FacultyOfColor #DontDoDartmouth" (5/13/2016). Her colleagues say Bahng stands out for her innovative work in Asian-American studies, for gaining national attention for leading a faculty collective on Black Lives Matter, and participating in a collaborative book project. Yet, it seems that she ran up against Dartmouth's "culture of politeness" and for confusing service with activism (Flaherty, 2016; Silverstein, 2016). Echoing Fryberg and Martínez's shrewd analysis of faculty of color as the university's convenient diversity jugglers, Professor Ellison voices her disillusionment with Dartmouth:

> Beyond tenure denials, some faculty members of color have left Dartmouth on their own. In a Facebook post about the departures, Treva C. Ellison, a lecturer in geography and women, gender, and sexuality studies,

wrote that the "lack of critical faculty here always means that any new person hired who can feel what direction gravity pulls in is going to be inundated with more work than their white cisgendered male counterparts and other zero-G hires." Dartmouth doesn't have a "diversity problem," she added, "rather, the temporary, precarious, and disavowed labor of people of color at Dartmouth is their purposeful and intentional diversity solution." (cited in Flaherty, 2016)

The neocolonial university relegates faculty of color to the ranks of precariate labor while showing off in glossy magazines that they are "doing diversity." This leaves junior faculty of color "with mixed messages and double standards, while the university gets to claim diversity as a core value" (Fryberg & Martínez, 2014, p. 8).

Inclusive excellence goals are still tenuous, especially in research universities which prize publication with certain publishing houses and journals; and they devalue faculty committed to action research and publish those in "low impact" journals. Faculty who pursue such work and still hope for tenure and promotion need to be mindful that service to the community and the profession does not really count towards enhancing their reputation. For some junior faculty of color it is simply impossible to pursue a false choice, i.e., of either being part of the struggle or being an acceptable public intellectual who will keep politics out of the classroom (June, 2015). With increasing attention to assessment, what can be said about something as simple as disaggregated recruitment and retention data of U.S. and international faculty of color? A data-driven university will cloak itself in silence over such simple analysis. Stephanie A. Fryberg and Ernesto J. Martínez (2014, p. 3) clarify: "With rare exceptions, universities frequently invoke narratives of progress in lieu of providing measurable outcomes (Moreno, Smith, Clayton-Pedersen, Parker, & Teraguchi, 2006). This often comes in the form of overidealizing administrative 'goodwill' and generalizing campus-wide 'efforts.'" Universities such as Yale are under increasing scrutiny why faculty of color are not receiving tenure. Often, Black Student Unions are driving this social justice call for action, unwilling to settle for empty gestures by administrators who favor discourses of equity and inclusion and cultural competence.

Fryberg and Martínez perceptively note another constraint imposed at research universities, which cannot break free from narrowly conceived academic standards:

> [W]omen of color feminism as a field of study would not have existed without the 1980s and 1990s institution-building labor of creating publishing houses like Third Woman Press and Kitchen Table Press. Groundbreaking volumes of interdisciplinary inquiry like *This Bridge Called My Back* (Moraga & Anzaldúa, 1981), *Making Face/ Making Soul* (Moraga & Anzaldúa, 1990), and *All the Women Are White, All the Men Are Black, but Some of Us Are Brave* (Hull, Scott, & Smith, 1982) might not have been published without these alternative publishing venues. More important, the methodologies that arose from these volumes—methodologies that now form the foundation of established schools of thought in the humanities and social sciences—would never have reached their paradigm-shifting potential, if these writers had waited to be published separately in journals or individual single-authored books. (2014, p. 7)

Never mind that these are now classic textbooks taught at research universities' feminist studies programs! Part of the paradigm shift is a nod towards the intersectionality of "unruly categories" (cf. Young, 1998) in contemporary North American feminist and critical race theoretical discourses, which are clearly indebted to the transformative texts by women of color. Recently, the progressive women of color INCITE! collective organized inspiring grassroots conferences and publishing activist-oriented books, e.g. *The Color of Violence* (2006). Their intersectional work helped make connections between the mutually reinforcing oppressive matrices of oppression, settler colonialism, racism, heterosexism, and that feminist work entails being vigilant about one's complicity with agents of the criminal justice complex. White feminist activists and scholars often failed to critique the role of police and social workers vis-à-vis stigmatized work, sexual violence, and relationship violence. Black Lives Matter's gender queer founders Alicia Garca, Patrisse Cullors, and Opal Tometi (Garca, 2014) brought to international attention what is at stake and with this new social movement were able to influence discussions in all sectors of society, including, of course, the university curriculum and social climate. BLM signifies the power of coupling the politics of recognition with the demands of structural change.

In these volatile times, college presidents and their diversity actors are advised to create real accountability measures on structural diversity questions, which clearly go beyond perfunctory celebrations of diversity or unity. In an environment of diversity management, they may ask themselves whether they can rely on the support of the institution's diversity officer who has been trained to diffuse resistant practices. Sara Ahmed (2012)'s advice is clear of what is the proper approach: "We might need to be the cause of obstruction. We might need to get in the way if we are to get anywhere. We might need to become the blockage points by pointing out the blockage points" (p. 187). Yet, so often, the academy leaves no room other than leaving one's post, as Sara Ahmed just did in May 2016. In her resignation letter she writes: "Sometimes we have to leave a situation because we are feminists. Wherever I am, I will be a feminist. I will be doing feminism. I will be living a feminist life. I will be chipping away at the walls." Arguably, "diverse" members of any campus community who face some or all aspects of the "five faces of oppression," outlined by Iris M. Young (1990), namely, powerlessness, exploitation, marginalization, cultural imperialism, violence, have little if anything to "gain" in a corporate model of "diversity management." The effective exclusion of their affective physical and emotional labor can be quite carefully managed under the elusive goal of diversity inclusion, access, and equity. Clearly, world-renowned Professor Sara Ahmed, Professor of Media and Communications and Director of the Centre for Feminist Research, did not feel included at Goldsmiths and as "feminist killjoy" scholar-activist certainly could not be "managed" within a risk-adverse institution.

Acknowledgments

Thanks to the anonymous reviewers of *Wagadu* and Nikita Dhawan's guidance on an earlier version of this paper. I am also grateful to Henry Steck for research assistance and discussion. All errors are mine.

References

Ahmed, S. (2012). *On being included: Racism and diversity in institutional life*. Durham: Duke University Press.

Ahmed, S. (2016). Resignation. Feminist killjoys blog. Retrieved from https://feministkilljoys.com/2016/05/30/resignation/

Alexander, M. (2010). *The new Jim Crow: Mass incarceration in the era of colorblindness*. New York: The New Press.

Banks, J.A. (2016). *Cultural diversity and education: Foundations, curriculum, and teaching* (6th ed.). New York: Routledge.

Bart, M. (2016). Diversity and inclusion in the college classroom: Special report. *Faculty Focus*. Retrieved from http://www.facultyfocus.com

Berkowitz, D. S. (1948). *Inequality of opportunity in higher education: A study of minority group and related barriers to college admission*. Albany: Williams Press.

Bigelow, B. & Peterson, B. (2003). *Rethinking Columbus*: A 500 Year History (2nd ed.). Rethinking Schools. Retrieved from http://www.rethinkingschools.org/ProdDetails.asp?ID=094296120X

Biondi, M. (2012). *The black revolution on campus*. Berkeley: University of California Press.

Black Liberation Collective (2015). Our principles. Retrieved from http://www.blackliberationcollective.org/our-beliefs/.

CCA (March 2015). Boxed out: Criminal history screening and college application attrition. Center for Community Alternatives. Retrieved 12/30/15 from: http://communityalternatives.org/pdf/publications/BoxedOut_FullReport.pdf

Churchill, W. (1998). White studies: The intellectual imperialism of US higher education. In C. Willett (Ed.), *Theorizing multiculturalism: A guide to the current debate.* Malden, MA: Blackwell.

Clark, J.B., Leslie, W. B. & O'Brien, K.P. (2010). *SUNY at sixty: The promise of the State University of New York.* Albany, NY: SUNY Press.

Cluster, D. (1979). The borning struggle: An interview with Bernice Johnson Reagon. Retrieved from http://civilrightsteaching.org/resource/the-borning-struggle-bernice-johnson-reagon/

Combahee River Collective (1977). The Combahee River Collective statement. Retrieved from http://circuitous.org/scraps/combahee.html.

Cox, Jr., T. (1991). The multicultural organization. *Academy of Management Executive, 5*(2), 34-47.

Cuomo, A. (3/29/2016). Governor Cuomo bans non-essential state travel to North Carolina. Governor A. Cuomo website. Retrieved from https://www.governor.ny.gov/news/governor-cuomo-bans-non-essential-state-travel-north-carolina

CUNY History (n.d.). The history of the City College of New York: 1969-1999. Retrieved from http://cunyhistory.tripod.com/thehistoryofcitycollege19691999/id1.html

CUNY Matters (10/12/2011). When CUNY was free, sort of. *CUNY Matters.* Retrieved from http://www1.cuny.edu/mu/forum/2011/10/12/when-tuition-at-cuny-was-free-sort-of/

Davis, A.Y. (1981). *Women, Race, and Class.* New York: Penguin

DiTomaso, N. (2013). *The American non-dilemma: Racial inequality without racism.* New York: Russell Sage Foundation.

DiversityInc (n.d.). "Things NOT to say" archives. Retrieved from http://www.diversityinc.com/topic/things-not-to-say/

Flaherty, C. (2016). Tenure denied. *Inside Higher Education.* Retrieved from https://www.insidehighered.com/news/2016/05/17/campus-unrest-follows-tenure-denial-innovative-popular-faculty-member-color

Fraser, N. (1998). From redistribution to recognition? Dilemmas of justice in a 'post-socialist' age. In C. Willett (Ed.), *Theorizing multiculturalism: A guide to the current debate.* Malden, MA: Blackwell.

Fryberg, S.A. & Martínez, E. J. (2014). Constructed strugglers. In S.A. Fryberg & E.J. Martínez (Eds.), *The truly diverse faculty: New dialogues in American higher education.* New York: Palgrave Macmillan.

Frye, M. (1983). Oppression. In *Politics of reality.* Trumansburg, NY: Crossing Press.

Gallagher, S. (2013). *Brothers of the black list.* Passion River Films.

Garza, A. (2015). Black lives matter. *The Feminist Wire.* Retrieved from http://www.thefeministwire.com/2014/10/blacklivesmatter-2/

Gladney, J. (11/20/2015). Black students who demand equality aren't impinging on your rights. *Occupy.Com.* Retrieved from http://www.occupy.com/article/black-students-who-demand-equality-arent-impinging-your-rights

Glazier, J. (1989). Nelson Rockefeller and the politics of higher education in New York State. In R. Geiger (Ed.), *History of Higher Education Annual*, vol. 9 (pp. 87-114). New Brunswick, NJ: Transaction Publishers.

Gonzalez, M. (2/3/2016). Finally, Europe is waking up to dangers of multiculturalism. *Daily Signal*. Retrieved from http://dailysignal.com/2016/02/03/finally-europe-is-waking-up-to-dangers-of-multiculturalism/

Hanson, H. (3/33/2016). Nixon aide reportedly admitted drug war was meant to target black people. *Huffington Post*. Retrieved from (http://www.huffingtonpost.com/entry/nixon-drug-war-racist_us_56f16a0ae4b03a640a6bbda1

Huntington, S. (1993). The clash of civilizations? *Foreign Affairs*, Summer. Retrieved from https://www.foreignaffairs.com/articles/united-states/1993-06-01/clash-civilizations

INCITE! Women of color against violence. (2006). *The color of violence: The INCITE! anthology*. Boston: South End Press.

June, A.W. (July 20, 2015). When activism is worth the risk. *Chronicle of Higher Education*. Retrieved from http://chronicle.com/article/When-Activism-Is-Worth-the/231729/

Kadi, J. (1996). *Thinking class: Sketches from a cultural worker*. Boston: South End Press.

Kelley, R. (3/7/2016). Forum: Black study, black struggle. *Boston Review*. Retrieved from https://bostonreview.net/forum/robin-d-g-kelley-black-study-black-struggle

King, M.L. (1963). "I have a dream ...". Retrieved from http://www.let.rug.nl/usa/documents/1951-/martin-luther-kings-i-have-a-dream-speech-august-28-1963.php

Kozol, J. (1991). *Savage inequalities: Children in America's schools*. New York: Random House.

Loewen, J. (1995). *Lies my teacher told me: Everything your American history textbook got wrong.* New York: Touchstone.

Lorde, A. (1983). There is no hierarchy of oppressions. *Bulletin: Homophobia and Education.* Retrieved from http://womenscenter.missouri.edu/wp-content/uploads/2013/05/THERE-IS-NO-HIERARCHY-OF-OPPRESSIONS.pdf

Mauer, M. (2006). *Race to incarcerate* (2nd ed.). New York: The New Press.

Moser, L. (10/15/2015). How did a Texas textbook end up describing slaves as "workers from Africa"? *The Slate.* Retrieved from http://www.slate.com/blogs/schooled/2015/10/06/texas_textbook_controversy_roni_dean_burren_finds_omission_in_son_s_geography.html

Nagel, M. & Asumah, S.N. (2014). Diversity studies and managing differences: Unpacking SUNY Cortland's case and national trends (pp. 349-466). In G. Hentges et al. (Eds.), *Sprache - Macht – Rassismus.* Berlin: Metropol Verlag.

Nagel, M. (2008). Prisons as diasporic sites: Liberatory voices from the diaspora of confinement. *Journal of Social Advocacy and Systems Change,* 1, March, 1-31.

Pager, D. (2004). The mark of a criminal record. *Focus,* 23(2), 44-46.

Paulson, A. (5/19/2010). Texas textbook war: "Slavery" or "Atlantic-triangular trade"? *The Christian Science Monitor.* Retrieved from

http://www.csmonitor.com/USA/Education/2010/0519/Texas-textbook-war-Slavery-or-Atlantic-triangular-trade

Peagler, R. (2000). Report: Recruitment and retention of ethnic minority students. SUNY Cortland. On file with author.

Perez, M. & Saldaña, J. (6/22/2016). Before we say "no more drug war," we need to say "black lives matter" and "not one more." Huffington Post. Retrieved from http://www.huffingtonpost.com/maritza-perez/no-more-drug-war-racism_b_10616636.html

Porter, N. (2016). Unfinished project of civil rights in the era of mass incarceration and the movement for black lives. *Wake Forest Journal of Law & Policy*, 6(1), 1-34. Retrieved from http://www.sentencingproject.org/publications/unfinished-project-of-civil-rights-in-the-era-of-mass-incarceration-and-the-movement-for-black-lives/

Prinster, R. (2016). University of Tennessee forced to shutter its diversity office. *Insight Into Diversity*. Retrieved from: http://www.insightintodiversity.com/university-of-tennessee-forced-to-shutter-its-diversity-office/

Reingold, J. (Jan. 21, 2015). Everybody hates Pearson. *Fortune*. Retrieved from http://fortune.com/2015/01/21/everybody-hates-pearson/

Renfro, S. & Armour-Garb., A. (1999). Report: Open admissions and remedial education at The City University of New York. Archives of Rudolph Giuliani. Retrieved from http://www.nyc.gov/html/records/rwg/cuny/pdf/history.pdf

Rothwell, J. (6/29/2016). Black and Latino kids get lower quality pre-K. Brookings Institution. Retrieved from http://www.brookings.edu/blogs/

Russell-Brown, K. (2008). *The color of crime: Racial hoaxes, white fear, black protectionism, police harassment, and other macroaggressions* (2nd ed.). New York: New York University Press.

Shermer, E.T. (2015). Nelson Rockefeller and the State University of New York's rapid rise and decline. Rockefeller Archive Center Research Reports Online. Retrieved from: http://www.rockarch.org/publications/resrep/shermer.pdf

Silverstein, H. (1/ 2016). Faculty panel discusses the teaching of "black lives matter." *Dartmouth Now*. Retrieved from http://now.dartmouth. edu/2016/01/faculty-panel-discusses-teaching-black-lives-matter

Steck, H. (2012). Higher education in New York. In G. Benjamin (Ed.), *The Oxford handbook on government in New York*. New York: Oxford University Press.

Steck, H. et al. (1992). Report: Toward a more equitable, inclusive, and diverse academic community. SUNY Cortland. (on file with author)

Takaki, R. (1993). *A different mirror: A multicultural history of the United States*. New York: Little, Brown.

Tauriac, J. & Liem, J. (2012). Exploring the divergent academic outcomes of U.S.-origin and immigrant-origin Black undergraduates. *Journal of Diversity in Higher Education*, 5(4): 10.1037/a0030181. Retrieved from http://www.ncbi.nlm.nih.gov/pmc/articles/PMC3816006/

The White House (6/11/2016). White House launches fair chance in higher education. *University Business Magazine*. Retrieved from http://www.universitybusiness.com/news/ white-house-launches-fair-chance-higher-education-pledge

Traub, J. (1994). *City on a hill: Testing the American dream at City College*. Reading, MA: Addison-Wesley.

Vertovec, S. (2014). Introduction: Formulating diversity studies. In S. Vertovec (Ed.), *Routledge international handbook on diversity studies* (pp. 1-20). London: Routledge.

Vollman, A. (5/26/2016). Pomona adds diversity requirement to tenure-review process. *Insight Into Diversity*. Retrieved from http://www.insightintodiversity.com/ pomona-college-adds-diversity-requirement-to-tenure-review-process/

Wallis, V. (2015). Intersectionality's binding agent: The political primacy of class. *New Political Science*, 37(4), 604-619.

Wilhelm, I. (4/17/2016). Why an armed occupation of Cornell in 1969 still matters today. *The Chronicle of Higher Education*. Retrieved from http://chronicle.com/article/Why-an-Armed-Occupation-of/236133

Wilson, J. (12/31/2015). How black lives matter saved higher education. *Al Jazeera America*. Retrieved from http://america.aljazeera.com/opinions/2015/12/how-black-lives-matter-saved-higher-education.html

Worthington, R., Stanley, C., & Lewis, W. (2014). Standards of Professional Practice for Chief Diversity Officers. National Association of Diversity Officers in Higher Education.

Wrench, J. (2014). Diversity management. In S. Vertovec (Ed.), *Routledge international handbook on diversity studies* (pp. 254-262). London: Routledge.

Young, I. M. (1990). *Justice and the politics of difference*. Princeton: Princeton University Press.

Young, I. M. (1998). Unruly categories: A critique of Nancy Fraser's dual systems analysis. In C. Willett (Ed.), *Theorizing multiculturalism: A guide to the current debate*. Malden, MA: Blackwell.

Zimpher, N. (September 10, 2015). Memorandum (re: Diversity, Equity, and Inclusion Policy.) Office of the Chancellor, The State University of New York. Retrieved from https://www.suny.edu/about/leadership/board-of-trustees/meetings/webcastdocs/Reso%20Tab%2005%20-%20Diversity,%20Equity,%20and%20Inclusion%20Policy.pdf

Zinn, H. (1980). *A people's history of the United States*. New York: HarperCollins.

FOUR

RETHINKING DIVERSITY IN ACADEMIC INSTITUTIONS – FOR A REPOLITICIZATION OF DIFFERENCE AS A MATTER OF SOCIAL JUSTICE

Vanessa Eileen Thompson
Goethe University Frankfurt am Main
and Veronika Zablotsky
University of California Santa Cruz

Correspondence: Vanessa Eileen Thompson, Goethe University Frankfurt am Main and Veronika Zablotsky, University of California Santa Cruz
thompson@em.uni-frankfurt.de; vzablots@ucsc.edu

Abstract

In recent years, the grammar of diversity led to neoliberal policy changes in German academia which distract from as well as reinscribe postcolonial power relations. What are the uses of diversity, and what is undone by the diversity paradigm? We offer a feminist postcolonial critique of some effects and pitfalls of diversity politics.

Rethinking Diversity in Academic Institutions

Over the past years, the grammar of diversity has entered the neoliberal university in Germany in an intensified way. This tendency becomes apparent in the proliferation of awareness trainings, statistical instruments, monitoring measures, as well as recruitment materials emphasizing diversity studies programs aiming to generate applicable policies. Taken together, these institutional developments circumscribe the rearticulations of a complex regulatory regime of difference and "equality" in the German context. In this article, we explore some dimensions of these rhetorical shifts as they apply to higher education, and argue that they indicate a broader turn from assimilatory policies of erasure and exclusion to the selective incorporation of what we call "differential human capital"[1] – namely differences constructed as commodifiable assets for the individual and the institution according to the aims and rationalities of the German state – to carve out a niche for itself in the age of neoliberal diversity.

The diversity discourse promotes a staging of difference for the benefit of institutional public relations. At best, the university is given a new face. At the same time, we are witnessing a turn to diversity as a scholarly concern, so that Diversity Studies as a field could establish itself as an "integrative approach in research" (Krell et al., 2007). It seems, however, that most publications coming out of this relatively new field in the German context are mainly oriented towards policy

---

1   We mobilize the theory of human capital in explicit reference to Michel Foucault's critique of neo-liberalism as the recoding of all spheres of human life and behavior as susceptible to economic analysis so that human activity becomes always already economic activity, hence individual and collective humanity, human capital (see Foucault 2008). We conceive of the notion of "differential human capital" as a way to flag both, the differential valorization of skills, traits, and characteristics, as well as the valorization of difference itself as inherent to neoliberal diversification strategies for more efficient value extraction.

recommendations, and looking to the application and management of diversity (see e.g. Weißbach et al., 2009). But what about the actual practices of knowledge production and educational curricula? What about institutional discriminatory effects and hegemonic power relations within the university?

Given that the debate over diversity in the German context is a fairly new phenomenon and has replaced the rather short-lived focus on multiculturalism, we trace how the concept as such entered German-speaking academic settings, proceed to critique its dominant forms of reception, and discuss some of its pitfalls from a postcolonial-feminist perspective. Overall, we argue in favor of a repoliticization of difference as a matter of social justice and political action. In this way, we offer a contribution towards the long-term project of the abolition of colonial-racializing, gendering, and sexualizing processes that reproduce forms of difference which we see as inextricably linked and interlocking. A relational matrix of power produces differently constituted, relational subject positions and subjectivities, engendering differentiated capabilities and attachments. We argue that the discourse of "diversity" objectifies relations of power and stabilizes them through neoliberal inclusion of figures of difference in ways that, as Angela Davis has argued, make no difference (Davis, 2013), while simultaneously perpetuating and stabilizing social injustices within the realms of higher education.

Between Neoliberal Educational Profitability and Equal Treatment Politics

With the move to internationalize production and services since (at least) the 1990s, the category "diversity" has circulated mainly as a managerial paradigm in hope of remaining competitive in the international market place of higher education. This marketization of higher education in particular (Gutiérrez-Rodríguez, 2015; Kauppinen, 2012; Massey, 2004) has fostered the incorporation of diversity policies that are at the center of the restructuring processes of the neoliberal university (Ahmed, 2012; Gutiérrez-Rodríguez, 2015).

The commodification and regulation of "human resources" within education takes place against the backdrop of postcolonial migration, apprehended through discourses of diversity, increased mobility for some recognized as assets, while not for others, and neoliberal globalization.[2] Those others of diversity are tolerated as "guests," and "welcomed" into the university, at best, as auditors in gestures of postcolonial benevolence. The marketization of education and the workings of academic capitalism (Rhoades & Slaughter, 2004) both draw on the grammar and logic of diversity policies as part of a management agenda for profitability. At the same time, the rhetoric of diversity with its inclusive aspirations emphasizes the neoliberal appreciation of "variety," advertises intercultural competency as an asset to business, and operates with the semantics of equal opportunity. Against this background of the ambivalence of neoliberal educational profitability and equal treatment politics, discussions on diversity within and beyond the university should be placed under critical scrutiny.

The idea of diversity management as such entered the German discourse on the initiative of business representatives drafting a so called "Charta of Diversity," which inserted the German word for "variety" (*Vielfalt*) into the economic paradigm of diversification. As of now, this advance by market actors gained symbolic support from the European commission, but there is no outline for its implementation which as so often depends solely on the good will of the signing parties. Quite explicitly, this document seeks profitable ways to utilize "dimensions of diversity" to gain access to new markets. Those different "dimensions" are discussed as neatly compartmentalized forms of difference. The "dimension" sexual orientation is discussed no further than just in a short but poignant

---

2   Neoliberal globalization, for the purpose of this article, is defined as a
     contextual articulation of free market governmental practices in times of
     globalization with varied and often contradictory social and political rule
     (Sparke, 2006; Mountz et al., 2015).

mention of "catchword pink marketing."[3] Not only is this an affirmative reference to the commercial exploitability of homonationalist processes of pinkwashing (Puar, 2007; Puar & Rai, 2002; SUSPECT, 2010), but also a blunt attempt to take money out of the pockets of GLB(T) clientele, imagined as mostly white and middle class citizens.

At the same time, the European Union put the bullet point "anti-discrimination" on the agenda of the German government, which led to the passing of the "General Equal Treatment Act" (AGG) in 2006. However, this step was the result of a lengthy process that endured several legislative periods as various drafts of the AGG were rejected and the European Union had to remind the German government several times of its responsibility to pass anti-discrimination laws (Lewicki, 2014). As legal scholar and critical race theorist Cengiz Barskanmaz argues (2008), the finalized legal document prohibits all forms of racialization – that is, in principle. However, there cannot be any doubt about the fact that social and institutional reality is very far from a meaningful freedom from racialization. Further, anti-discrimination organizations have emphasized severe gaps in the institutionalization of the AGG. While policies and regulations across the member states of the European Union are more and more orchestrated and streamlined, the Republic of Germany has been admonished several times for its weak commitment to anti-racism, most recently in the reports of the European commission against racism and intolerance in Europe.[4]

The European Union as a supranational formation with the pretension of inclusiveness is mastering the language of diversity, as is already

---

3   http://www.charta-der-vielfalt.de/diversity/diversity-dimensionen/ sexuelle-orientierung.html (accessed in February 2016).

4   http://www.faz.net/aktuell/politik/europaeische-union/ fremdenfeindlichkeit-europarat-ruegt-mildes-vorgehen-gegen-rassismus-12819670.html (accessed in July 2015).

apparent in the choice of its leitmotif "United in Diversity,"[5] albeit for some and not for the majority of others. The mythologized "founding moment" of a newly conceived German Republic, the so called "German reunification," effectively remade Germany into a nation-state unified in homogeneity in addition to the administrative extension of the basic constitutional law of the Federal Republic of Germany to the territory of the former socialist German Democratic Republic. This conception effectively foreclosed the possibility of "diversity" for its subject population,[6] and lent rationality to the increasing effort to fortify impermeable border zones through the state-sanctioned murderous practices of private security agency Frontex.

In the media staging of a spectacularized "refugee crisis," really a crisis of European border regimes, over the past several years, the self-image of Germany as a tolerant, "welcoming" nation-state has been contrasted by frequent right-wing attacks on encampments and asylums haphazardly and precariously housing those seeking refuge from civil war and economic devastation elsewhere. The reemergence of the term "xenophobia" in German media – coded as the "fear of strangers," rather than racism – to explain increasingly hysterical and violent responses to both, asylum seekers and Germans of color, reinscribes the idea of all Germans as only white. The tendency to homogenize inwards and repel outwards is now aggravated in a German-led push to create an EU border fortification agency endowed with the sovereign authority to override particular nation-states unable or unwilling to fortify their borders against those seeking admission into the EU territory.

The German approach to difference can be described as a preference for homogenization and assimilation, understood as erasure or

---

5   http://europa.eu/about-eu/basic-information/symbols/motto/index_en.htm (accessed in February 2016).

6   The period of the early 1990s was characterized by racist pogroms which were "addressed" by deportations of the victims by the German government (see Ha, 2012).

domestification. The short-lived turn to "multiculturalism" as a framework to come to terms with the presence and social contributions of racialized subjects in Germany – Germans of color, or self-identifying in other terms, such as people of color, post-migrants, "Kanacks," "Ausländer," etc. – may have been quickly discarded, but its core idea of "Fördern und Fordern" (roughly translating to "support and demand") lives on under the umbrella of "integration politics" as a long-term concern of the German government. The trope of integration presupposes a preexisting, homogenous (white) German social body into which "foreigners" are expected to "integrate," preferably by assimilating to the German "Leitkultur," a neologism designating "German culture" as an organic, exemplary, and primary unit. In recent debates, assimilation seems to have become somewhat discredited, giving way to the idea of unconditional allegiance to the German constitution and mastery of the German language as prime indicators of "fitness" for presence and social participation in German society. Integration politics and the politics of diversity share a bureaucratic and governmental logic which further makes representation appear so desirable although it ultimately only strengthens the narrative of ownership that flows from the projection of nationalist discourses onto German citizenship and the German constitution – "Volk" and "völkisch" in the racialist sense.

At the present moment, we observe a rhetorical shift towards managerial and humanitarian diversity schemes as a new hegemonic discourse in the German context. Homogeneity is now recoded as an alleged cultural allegiance to values of tolerance and equality as a backdrop against which difference is sought to be neutralized through individual intimidation, cooptation, incorporation, and commodification according to the promise of value extraction for institutions, and the German national project more broadly construed. Given the absence of a serious debate about social justice understood in the sense of political negotiation and contestation instead of harmonization of political conflicts, we posit that exclusionary dynamics are articulated through a corporate lens of incorporation. Accordingly, the economic strategy of "diversification" for value creation has expanded into the sphere of higher education.

Diversity appears on the scene as a managerial discourse, which injects a certain "cosmopolitan" air of elite mobility and individual flexibility into an academic and white-collar sub-segment of integration politics – "diversifying" it, perhaps.

In debates about non-discrimination, equal treatment is understood, at best, as a form of compensation. More often, however, it is reduced to a notion of relief from unequal treatment for the individual, which misses layers of systemic and institutionalized exclusions within a relational field of power that renders attempts at equalization inconsequential. As long as anti-discrimination continues to be reduced to symbolic stagings of inclusion that are effectively non-performative (Ahmed, 2012), institutional logics and discourses are not only left intact, but also shielded and withdrawn from further political negotiations so that racialization becomes revalorized as the profitable basis of diversity.

Diversity as a Tool for Non-Discriminatory Higher Education?

The so-called "excellence initiative" of the German federal state and states is a major vehicle for the insertion of the diversity discourse into the German system of higher education since 2005. This orchestrated reform program explicitly posits the "internationalization" of universities as a criterion for funding decisions, which means that "future viability" ("*Zukunftstauglichkeit*") is understood as increased international competitiveness of Germany as a location for business and industry ("*Standort Deutschland*").[7] Thus, the question of the appeal of German knowledge production for the "global market of education" ("*weltweiter Bildungsmarkt*") is foregrounded.

It becomes apparent that the German system of higher education is reformed to replicate the North American context as spelled out in the

---

7   http://www.dfg.de/en/research_funding/programmes/excellence_ initiative/institutional_strategies/index.html (accessed in February 2016).

Bologna agreement (1999) which introduced a European three-year modularized Bachelor's degree for the sake of creating EU-wide quality standards in higher education (see Alesi & Kehm, 2010; Gutiérrez-Rodríguez, 2015), also by making funding decisions conditional on structural adjustments in the organization of knowledge production. Diversity as a "best practice solution" has thus traveled as an integral part of commodified university education.

In light of the colonial continuities undergirding globalization, the logic of development and progress is applied in differential ways. Previous notions of non-discrimination in the German university typically avoided the problem of institutionalized relations of inequality by placing the burden of compensation squarely on the shoulders of those affected by their consequences. The shift towards diversity further extends this logic by prescribing both, problem and solution. It should also be mentioned that the concept is in itself based on constitutive exclusions, since only those who have already secured their residence title or German citizenship can hope to be recognized as viable human capital by neoliberal(izing) institutions, diversity practitioners, and the state. The discourse around diversity in higher education is overall determined by a force field between neoliberal exploitation and equal treatment policies, delineated by overlapping discursive formations of harmonization and cooptation that operate in marked opposition to critiques of power.

For this reason, we now turn to our assessment of the multi-layered effects of diversity politics in the context of the neoliberal university, and to our critique of the dangers of its expansion without further scrutiny. To be sure, concepts of diversity may vary across fields of signification, so that the following may not necessarily apply at all times. However, we see crucial pitfalls even with diversity approaches that consider multidimensional forms of subjugation. We also distance ourselves from hegemonic appropriations of intersectional analysis that may pay lip service but fail to politically attend to the inextricability of categories of power by celebrating essentialist identity

politics or flattening power relations (Bilge, 2013; Erel et al., 2008).
When postcolonial/neoliberal governmentality of diversity operates
with "mix-and-stir" logic, intersectionality as a concept lends itself
to hegemonic universalizations (Dhawan & Castro Varela, 2009).
The staging or speaking of "variety" thus becomes a "happy point," a
polemic term coined by Sara Ahmed (2012, p. 14), to distract from the
socio-economic context in which diversity is set to work to foreclose
political practice.

Diversity as Distraction from and Reinscription of Postcolonial Relations of Power

The agenda of diversity in the new paradigmatic shift towards value
extraction from equality discourses has been extensively critiqued by
feminists of color in and outside the German context (Alexander, 2005;
Davis, 1996; Eggers, 2011; Haritaworn, 2012; Mohanty, 2003; Puwar,
2004, to name just a few). Despite their differences, they commonly
emphasize that discourses of diversity foster a disarticulation of power
relations that are distracted from in the very same moves that reproduce
and stabilize them. In our reflections, we tie in with some already
existing critiques to discuss the consequences of the boom of diversity
(without difference) in German universities. We begin by interrogating
the grammar of "variety" for its silences to show what the alleged
"mainstreaming" of diversity obscures.

Diversity is not only imagined in reports and drafts, but is also part of
representational regimes of legal ordering, calculation, and regulation.
We argue that this circumscribes the problematics of *reification and
appropriation* of difference. In her empirical work on diversity politics
and practices at universities in the British context, Sara Ahmed describes
how the representational "diversity mosaic" estranges racialized,
gendered, and sexualized subjects on all levels of the university (2012).
Diversity, here, means the selective inclusion of the Other-ed in its
commodity form – meaning, those produced, seen, and treated as

"different" in the focal point of the gendered/gendering and sexualized/sexualizing gaze.

The turn to the topic of diversity mainstreaming in the to-be-diversified and reconfigured German academic industrial complex is structured along a similar dynamic which reifies hegemonic centers and leaves them intact in the process of standardization and display of purported variety. A necessary condition for diversity, in this sense, is an assumed neutral position from which the ones other-ed are seen as "diverse." Maisha Eggers speaks in this context of the re-centering of hegemonic positions through the reification of "diversity creatures" (2011). With the resurrection of the German distinction between "guests" and "hosts," German subjects with "migration background" become potential ambassadors of integration and diversity in order to prove their allegiance to "democratic" values, which, in turn, is always already in question.

A further effect of the workings of diversity can be sketched out as *exclusionary inclusion* which fosters the *disarticulation of local critiques.* Oftentimes we incorporate critical voices from primarily Anglophone contexts in ways that are selective and reductive. This effectively amounts to a form of avoidance to engage with interventions in the German context and thus obfuscates the ways in which historically specific relations of power persist while presumably covered (but really, covered up) by diversity. After all, why is it institutionally encouraged to invite scholars of color as experts on oppression and struggles elsewhere when it is still so difficult to stage critical interventions by local scholars of color addressing and theorizing the German context? While transnational dialogues and solidarity are crucially important, we also want to point out that there is a dynamic of *exclusionary inclusion* at work that is problematic because it furthers the *disarticulation of local critiques.*

The critical archives of resistance by people of color (racialized people in the German context) are hence disqualified as what Jin Haritaworn has termed "pre-theoretical raw material" (2012, p.16). This raw material then, at best, circulates through channels of transnational recycling processes traveling back in the form of Anglophone publications (Bilge, 2013; Gutiérrez Rodríguez, 2010) and almost never makes it into German curricula where postcolonial, race critical theories, and non-Western knowledges are already placed at the margins, rendered further "empirical" material. To give an example, significant contributions by Black feminists and feminists of color to the debates about intersectionality in the German context in the 1980s continue to go ignored for the most part. Furthermore, queer and trans* Black people and people of color in Germany have articulated critiques of homonationalism and the multi-faceted forms of discrimination ("*Mehrfachdiskriminierung*") that too easily fall away in the perpetual pointing to an "elsewhere" (see, for example, SUSPECT, 2010). These interventions push back against the hegemonic desire to do away with allegations of racism in the German context. Tightly interwoven with these ideas about diversity as internationalization is, furthermore, their marked *arbitrariness* (is everything diverse?). Eggers reminds us that:

> When all forms of discrimination are simultaneously spoken about, it can happen quickly that all the speakers see themselves as equally discriminated against and lose sight of their own dominance with respect to other structural categories (Eggers, 2011, pp. 259-260).[8]

Moreover, the diversity discourse constructs and excludes those whose differences are seen as unassimilable to the molds of diversity – those are the "*Others of diversity*." Hence, only exploitable (read, assimilable and reified) forms of difference are deemed adequate to the variables of variety as defined in the managerial diversity manuals. This expansion of market logic aims to harmonize potentially conflictual dissimilarities by analogizing them, adding them up in a string in order to ingest and incorporate them as "diversity." Divergence is rendered a "harmless

---

8   Translation ours.

variation" in a move to replace political negotiations of historically sedimented relations of power through an empty pluralism (Mohanty, 2003, p.193).

A crucial element of this logic of a "diverse asset class"[9] is the simultaneous exclusion of those others of diversity who are classified as unmarketable, costly, or even threatening – perceived as unskilled, uneducated, intolerant, sexually aggressive, potentially terrorist, or seeking asylum "solely" for economic reasons.[10] Racism in all its variegated, subtle, and less subtle manifestations is rarely understood as a matter of importance to the Bureaus dealing with issues of unequal treatment institutionalized at most German universities. International offices mostly engender and enable migration regulations instead of countering institutional racism that international students from the Global South are exposed to (Gutiérrez Rodríguez, 2015). In fact, in most German universities there are no institutional resources for students, faculty staff, administrative and service staff who are confronted with racist, queer- and/or trans*-phobic forms of violence. Instead, this everyday violence is construed as exceptional. The rhetoric of diversity is contributing to the silencing of these forms of institutionalized violence which operate within the neoliberal university. The structural connections and ordinariness of institutionalized racism, queer- and transphobia, economic exploitation

---

9   http://www.charta-der-vielfalt.de/fileadmin/user_upload/beispieldateien/ Bilddateien/Publikationen/ Fl%C3%BCchtlinge_in_den_Arbeitsmarkt_-_Charta_der_ Vielfalt_2015.pdf (accessed in February 2016).

10 By means of the legal construct of "safe countries of origin," EU and national immigration policies have created a tool to demarcate who is a "refugee" in need of protection, and who an "economic migrant" ineligible for asylum, first and foremost by narrowly interpreting what constitutes "persecution." For a list of countries currently classified as "safe," see: http://ec.europa.eu/dgs/home-affairs/what-we-do/policies/ european-agenda-migration/background-information/docs/2_eu_safe_ countries_of_origin_de.pdf (accessed February 2016).

of labor that is devalued in racist and sexist ways, the systematic dehumanization through racist police violence, racial profiling, state sanctioned racist murders, genocidal border regimes, practices of deportation as well as regimes of incarceration and patronizing care are simply bracketed as irrelevant to questions of diversity in the university.

Against this backdrop, merely a naming and orderly display of diversity is not sufficient. In the search for "instruments" to improve on diversity in order to compete internationally, or to attract and recruit "international talent" – understood through the prism of postcolonial migration regulations that stratify international students (and staff) alongside postcolonial North-South relations through visa restrictions, limitations on work hours while simultaneously having to prove a yearly income through a bank statement, and requirements to enroll in German classes (even if the study programs are in English language) (see Gutiérrez Rodríguez, 2015). Academic institutions are caught up in ineffective bureaucratic procedures that are only productive in the sense that they create neatly compartmentalized silos of difference that operate without reference to the broader informal, economic, and legal dynamics that produce them. This posits difference as essence rather than an effect of relations of domination and oppression that mark people as "different" in ways that are experienced as violence. Based on this production of difference, subject and subjugated positions are ascribed. We should not forget that access to material and symbolic resources is already a complicating factor, even prior to any considerations of enrollment at the university (Nguyen, 2013). In focusing on individual privileges, scholars and some activists may risk ending up with a reductive critique of privilege that misses the point. As scholars embedded with and informed by activist practices and discourses, we have come to think of "privilege" not as something inherent, though it does shape subjectivity, create expectations towards a "good" future and happiness, and distribute intensities in socially produced space. These spaces of privilege take on the forms of some, making it harder for Others to enter and navigate this experience of densities. Privilege describes a condition that flows from cumulative processes of *privileging* with whiteness as its unmarked center.

In how far is it possible to bring about social justice as a meaningful, substantive transformation of these processes while neither erasing nor reifying difference? Are currently existing mechanisms of equal opportunity ("*Gleichstellung*") and equal treatment ("*Gleichbehandlung*") adequate to the task at hand of dissolving hegemonic centers? Diversity as individual inclusion instrumentalizes "variety" and erases the political need for anti-discrimination *to work*. Given this tendency, the diversity discourse runs the risk of leading to depoliticized identity politics (see e.g. Mohanty, 2003). For this reason, we argue that commodifying the idea of "identity" cannot in itself lead to meaningful social transformation, though it can serve as a heuristic means to address the effects of relations of production.

Towards a Repoliticization of Difference as a Matter of Social Justice

The exploitational administration of variety and the lip service to "diversity mainstreaming" is not only *not going far enough*, but all too easily misses the point. Too often we fail to problematize the ways in which practices of diversity categorically exclude persons without residency permits. One of many instances in the resurrection of the difference between "guests" and "hosts" are, for example, new initiatives in light of the so called "refugee crisis" to allow refugees to audit lectures in German universities – not for credit, but as a charitable form of diversion. Variety as a cross-cutting theme might put the problem of discriminatory relations on the agenda. It remains questionable, however, if a discourse coming from neoliberal business management and the individualization of political struggles over social justice is really suited to pave the way for the kinds of social transformations that are undoubtedly necessary to effectively counter current forms of exclusion, exploitation, exoticization, cooptation, and dehumanization.

What would be possible alternative strategies to further a long-term dismantling of structurally anchored subjugation in German society in general and in its universities in particular? Instead of attempting to neutralize contentious issues and possible lines of conflict by means of administrative logic and managerial discourse, we argue that their complex interwovenness should be robustly historicized, contextualized, and problematized in order to confront them within a framework of sustained political negotiation at all levels of society. This is what we conceptualize as social justice, defined as a political process of contestation in continued political struggles over processes of deliberation and harmonization with their effects of concealed asymmetrical relations. This includes an uncompromising and critical assessment of the incorporation of modes of social justice within the workings of power in its neoliberal and professionalized versions. Political negotiation also has to entail a serious engagement with the critiques and perspectives of those who are produced as Others at the conjunctures of racializing, gendering, and sexualizing processes, refracted by socio-economic capital, without essentializing their experience as a static feature of their "identities." It might even have to start with a close account of who it is that really emerges as *intelligibly other* in the first place to arrive at a form of postcolonial-feminist immanent critique[11] and articulations of social justice that shed light on forms of investment in Otherness at the expense of forms of difference that (have to) fall away to make space on the stage of diversity in the name of recognition. We conclude that forms of critique are asked for that decenter and destabilize the individual and challenge national border regimes. This would mean to ask questions about systemic and institutionalized violence as effects of power relations and to put diversity discourses under closer scrutiny as neoliberal versions of the nexus between the human and capital.

---

11 We conceive of a feminist postcolonial modality of immanent critique as both a form of assessment and evaluation in the sense of the Frankfurt School as well as a critique of its immanent criteria.

Acknowledgements

We would like to thank Nikita Dhawan for her kind encouragement to draft a version of our paper presented at the International Workshop of the Frankfurt Research Center for Postcolonial Studies in February 2015 into the current article. Her generous comments and the valuable feedback of two anonymous reviewers were instrumental in strengthening our argument. Our conversation has been ongoing since Angela Y. Davis' visit at the Goethe University Frankfurt am Main in December 2013 which inaugurated the Chair in International Gender and Diversity Studies in her name at the Cornelia Goethe Centrum for Women and Gender Studies. We thank Noa Ha and Jin Haritaworn for initiating and inspiring our collaboration on the politics of diversity in German academia and beyond. This article represents an ongoing transnational conversation, a version of which is also forthcoming in German language in the dossier "Geschlossene Gesellschaft?" of the Heinrich Böll Foundation, edited by Kien Nghi Ha, Noa Ha, and Mekonnen Mesghena. Many thanks also to Smaran Dayal, Kira Kosnick, Sara Salem, and Alexander Vorbrugg for valuable comments.

References

Ahmed, S. (2012). *On being included. Racism and diversity in institutional life*. Durham/London: Duke University Press.

Alexander, J. M. (2005). *Pedagogies of crossing: Meditations on feminism, sexual politics, memory, and the sacred*. Durham/London: Duke University Press.

Barskanmaz, C. (2008). Rassismus, Postkolonialismus und Recht - Zu einer deutschen Critical Race Theory? *Kritische Justiz*, 3, 296-302.

Bilge, S. (2013). Intersectionality undone. Saving Intersectionality from Feminist Intersectionality Studies. *Du Bois Review, 10 (2)*, 405–424.

Davis, A. Y. (2013). Inaugural Speech for the Angela Davis Guest Professorship at Cornelia Goethe Centrum of Goethe Universität Frankfurt. Retrieved from http://www.cgc.uni-Frankfurt.de/feminismabolition.shtml

Dhawan, N. & Castro Varela, M. M. (2009). Mission Impossible? Postkoloniale Theorie im deutschsprachigen Raum. In: J. Reuter, & P.-I. Villa (Eds.), *Postkoloniale Soziologie. Theoretische Anschlüsse - Empirische Befunde - politische Interventionen* (pp. 239-260). Bielefeld: transcript.

Eggers, M. M. (2011). Diversität. In S. Arndt, & N. Ofuatey-Rahal (Eds.), *Wie Rassismus aus Wörtern spricht, (K)Erben des Kolonialismus im Wissensarchiv deutsche Sprache* (pp.254-261). Münster: Unrast.

Erel, U., Haritaworn, J., Gutiérrez Rodríguez, E., & Klesse, C. (2008). On the depoliticization of intersectionality talk: Conceptualizing multiple oppressions in critical sexuality studies. In A. Kuntsman, & E. Miyake (Eds.): *Out of place: Interrogating silences in queerness/raciality* (pp. 265–292). New York: Raw Nerve Books.

Foucault, Michel (2008). *The Birth of Biopolitics: Lectures at the Collège de France, 1978-1979.* New York: Picador.

Gutiérrez-Rodríguez, E. (2010). Decolonizing postcolonial rhetoric. In E. Gutiérrez Rodríguez, M. Boatca, & S. Costa (Eds.), *Decolonizing European sociology: Transdisciplinary approaches* (pp. 49–70). Farnham, UK: Ashgate.

Gutiérrez-Rodríguez, E. (2015). Sensing dispossession: Women and gender studies between institutional racism and migration control policies in the neoliberal university. *Women's Studies International Forum,* 1-11.

Haritaworn, J. (2012). *The biopolitics of mixing: Thai multiracialities and haunted ascendancies.* Farnham, UK: Ashgate.

Kauppinen, I. (2012). Towards transnational academic capitalism. *Higher Education,* 64(4), 543–556.

Kien, N. (2012). *Rostock-Lichtenhagen – Die Rückkehr des Verdrängten.* Retrieved from http://asiatischedeutsche.wordpress.com/2012/09/19/rostock-lichtenhagen-die-ruckkehr-des-verdrangten/

Krell, G., Riedmüller, B., Sieben, B., & Vinz, D. (Eds.) (2007). *Diversity Studies. Grundlagen und disziplinäre Ansätze.* Frankfurt am Main: Campus.

Lewicki, Aleksandra (2014). Allgemeines Gleichbehandlungsgesetz: Zwischenbilanz eines brüchigen Konsenses. Retrieved from http://www.bpb.de/apuz/180859/allgemeines-gleichbehandlungsgesetz-zwischenbilanz-eines-bruechigen-konsenses?p=all

Massey, D. (2004). Geographies of responsibility. *Geografiska Annaler: Series B, Human Geography, 86(1),* 5–18.

Mohanty, C. T. (2003). *Feminism without borders. Decolonizing theory, practicing solidarity.* Durham/London: Duke University Press.

Mountz, A., Bonds, A., Mansfield, B., Loyd, J., Hyndman, J., Walton-Roberts, & Curran, W. (2015). For a slow scholarship: A feminist politics of resistance through collective action in the neoliberal university. *ACME: An International E-Journal for Critical Geographies, 14(4),* 1235 - 1259.

Nguyen, T. Q. (2013). Schulisch-institutionelle Rassismuserfahrungen, kindliche Vulnerabilität und Mikroaggression. *Zeitschrift für internationale Bildungsforschung und Entwicklungspädagogik, 36 (2),* 20-24.

Puar, J. (2007) *Terrorist assemblages. Homonationalism in queer times.* Durham/London: Duke University Press.

Puar, J. and A. Rai (2002) Monster, terrorist, fag: The war on terrorism and the production of docile patriots. *Social Text 72,* 20(3), 117-148.

Puwar, N. (2004). *Space invaders: Race, gender and bodies out of place.* London, UK: Berg Publishers.

Rhoades, G., & Slaughter, S. (2004). *Academic capitalism in the new economy: Challenges and choices.* Baltimore, MD: The John Hopkins University Press.

Sparke, M. (2006). A neoliberal nexus: Economy, security, and the biopolitics of citizenship at the border. *Political Geography, 25(2),* 151-180.

SUSPECT (2010.06.26). Where now? From pride scandal to transnational movement. Retrieved from http://bullybloggers. wordpress.com/2010/06/26/where-now-from-pride-scandal-to-transnational-movement/

Weißbach, B., Weißbach, H.-J., & Kipp, A. (2009). *Managing Diversity. Konzepte – Fälle – Tools. Ein Trainings-Handbuch.* Dortmund: BWV.

FIVE

EXPOSING THE THREADS: A CRITICAL INTERROGATION OF THE POLICIES, PRACTICES AND (NON-) PERFORMATIVITY OF DIVERSITY IN THE CITY OF TORONTO

Shana Almeida
York University, Toronto, Ontario, Canada

Correspondence: Shana Almeida, Department of Social Work, Trent University, Peterborough, Ontario
shanaalmeida@trentu.ca

Abstract

This paper explores "diversity" as a discourse, and thus as a mechanism of power. Specifically, this paper invites a critical interrogation into the racial logics of diversity and how political power of government and its policies have been constructed through race, which in turn binds the racialized body against the changing landscape of the City.

Introduction

The language of diversity is elusive, pervasive, and widely contested. For some, diversity is a celebration of multi-cultures; for others, diversity reinforces racial lines, whiteness, and racism. Over the past two decades, multiculturalism scholars have argued that diversity inspires pluralism as well as inclusive policies and practices which seek to accommodate equal recognition of cultural identities in order to transcend the boundaries of difference (see for example Good, 2009; Isin & Siemiatycki, 1997; Kymlicka, 1995; Kymlicka & Banting, 2006; Nagle, 2009; Parekh, 2006). Yet critical race scholars also contend that celebrations of cultural "difference," proclamations of political success, and feelings of happiness and harmony that diversity inspires conceal the centrality of race and power in its construction (see Ahmed, 2000, 2012; Bannerji, 2000; Cross & Keith, 1993; Jordan & Weedon, 2015; Keith, 2002; Puwar, 2004; Shaw, 2007). In short, conceptualizations of what diversity is, or what it *does,* are riddled with tensions and contradictions.

These contradictions are highlighted further in empirical studies of diversity in the City of Toronto,[1] a municipal government which claims that Toronto is "one of the most diverse cities in the world and has gained an international reputation for the successful management of its diversity" (City of Toronto, 2003a, p. 2). The City of Toronto's motto "Diversity Our Strength" implies a celebration of ethnic harmony and multicultural inclusion in a city that is now over fifty percent people of color (Altilia, 2003; Boudreau, Keil & Young, 2009; Saloojee & Siemiatycki, 2002). In her study of how responsive Canadian municipalities are to their multicultural communities, Kristen Good (2009) suggests that the official adoption of the City of Toronto's diversity motto is one example of how integral the accommodation, integration, and engagement with immigrant and ethno-cultural groups are to the City's mandate and image. In Good's view, initiatives such as these show

---

1   Big "C" City refers to the corporation/municipal government, small "c" city to the metropolis.

how the City of Toronto goes "well beyond their limits" to respond to and successfully "manage its diversity" (p. 87). As she also suggests, it is evident that diversity and multiculturalism are extremely important to the City of Toronto, as "community leaders representing immigrants and ethnocultural minorities would not support an increased municipal role in immigrant settlement and multiculturalism policy if the city were not responsive to their concerns" (p. 65).

However, empirical studies which link diversity with race and/or racism in the City of Toronto indicate that despite the motto, the City has consistently excluded racialized communities from its political decision-making processes (Altilia, 2003). In her study of the City of Toronto, Carol Altilia (2003) argues that diversity precludes analyses of inequity, and as such, the exclusion of racialized communities in Toronto's municipal government is not prioritized, or even addressed (Altilia, 2003). As Sheila Croucher (1997) also points out, because the City of Toronto relies heavily on its image as a "diverse" city of multiple languages, cultures, and positive ethnic relations to compete effectively in the global marketplace, any struggles based on race and class are effectively written out of the historical and political space of the city.

How is it possible for the term "diversity" in the City of Toronto to vacillate between presence *and* absence, inclusion *and* exclusion, mobilization *and* repression of racialized communities? Furthermore, under what condition(s) might any tensions between the "inclusion" of bodies and the "management" of bodies dissolve to a point where they appear in a natural, even symbiotic relationship? This paper takes these paradoxical moments as its point of departure. Specifically, in this paper I seek to demonstrate how diversity, as a discourse and as a mechanism of power, negotiates and transforms multiple conceptual, racial, and embodied schisms into the re-production and justification of particular historical "truths" and knowledge which provide the conditions for the possibility and (re-)emergence of diversity in the present. As Michel Foucault (1984) writes, in understanding discourse, we must seek to understand, historically, how truth and its effects are produced within discourses which accept and make it function as truth. Discourse thus provides "the mechanisms and instances which enable one to distinguish true and false statements, the means by which each is sanctioned; the techniques and procedures accorded value in the acquisition of truth; the status of those who are charged with saying what counts as true" (Foucault, 1984, p. 73). As Ann Laura Stoler (1995) also argues, power organizes "truths" (or truth-claims) in a way that justifies and re-produces historical, social, and racial distinctions and exclusions in the world. This paper begins to trace the historical and racial conditions, practices, and truth-claims which rearticulate and are rearticulated by diversity discourse in the City of Toronto, in order to begin to grasp the political force behind truth, knowledge, and diversity itself.

Attending to the Local – Diversity and Space

There are multiple and in some cases conflicting interpretations of the relationship between the municipality and the central state on conceptualizations of diversity and race. Malcolm Cross and Michael Keith (1993) argue that it is both politically and theoretically necessary to interrogate whether the limits of "race equality" efforts in Cities, as far as they may have been pushed, reflect the extent of the commitments made by municipalities themselves, or "the degree to which the mirage of an autonomous urban political machine masked the necessary subservience of the local to the central state" (p. 20). Scholarly research in this area demonstrates the complex interplay of factors that make interpreting and taking up this task a challenge.

In the City of Toronto, diversity policies and practices are often directly linked to liberal state multiculturalism and its celebrations of ethnic differences that have dominated Canadian public discourse for years (Boudreau, Keil & Young, 2009; Catungal & Leslie, 2009; Croucher 1997; Good, 2009; Goonewardena & Kipfer, 2005). Julie-Anne Boudreau, Roger Keil and Douglas Young (2009) suggest that although Toronto offers serious challenges to the multiculturalism policies of the nation-state in terms of the actual lived experiences of 'visible minorities' and the anti-racist actions that are sparked by them, multiculturalism remains central to the City's various "diversity actions"(p. 88)[2]. Kanishka Goonewardena and Stefan Kipfer (2005) and Croucher (1997) further suggest that bourgeois urbanism uses multiculturalism in Canada to reinforce capitalist urbanization and the desires of the elite and middle class because of its occlusion of the racial hierarchies and nationalist narratives that constitute and are re-constituted by multiculturalism policies. Multicultural rhetoric thus allows Toronto as an urban setting to re-imagine itself as ethnically harmonious while preventing racism from being seen as a social problem (Croucher, 1997). Croucher (1997) espouses that the idea of urban ethnic relations being harmonious in Toronto largely serves the interests of elites (including those of the local state), who use the ideology of multiculturalism in order to demonstrate the irrelevance of race and racism in Toronto, and to its municipal government. For those who suggest that the City of Toronto's diversity policies draw directly from Canada's multiculturalism policies, they tend to gradually conflate diversity and multiculturalism, and present the diversity policies of the City of Toronto and Canadian multicultural policies as essentially accomplishing the same thing. This begs the question: why "Diversity Our Strength" in the City of Toronto, and not simply "Multicultural(ism) Our Strength?"

In this paper, I pay close attention to the specificities of diversity discourse in the City of Toronto, following Jane M. Jacob's (1996) assertion that the local space of the city, as a site of contemporary close(r) encounters with the racial Other, re-produces imperial anxieties which has particular implications for the making of subjects. Although there has been a significant focus on how race is experienced and negotiated in Toronto, significantly less attention has been paid to what the City of Toronto's diversity policies and practices actually *do* with these anxieties, as well as *with, for and to the racial bodies that produce them*. In this vein, I move away from attempts to capture how the City's diversity policies might (or might not) reflect the multiculturalism policies of the nation-state, and

---

2   In fact, the authors refer to the City's diversity policies as "multicultural policies." (p. 88)

instead pursue critical questions of what diversity discourse does in and for the City of Toronto, *as a specific and local context.*

Sherene Razack (2002) also asks that we pay close attention to the co-constitution of bodies and spaces, as well to the colonial and racist discourses that produce and contain "how subjects come to know themselves in and through space" (p. 17). In my analyses, I begin to trace how increasing encounters with racial Others evoke specific spatial and racial anxieties which are recuperated via diversity discourse in the City of Toronto, to reproduce processes of inclusion, exclusion, and subjectivity in racial terms. I also show how racial subjects in the City are discursively produced and contained via diversity to simultaneously reproduce the City as a "leader" in addressing issues of diversity and racism. This paper thus poses some important questions about the role of diversity discourse in the co-production of race, space, and the racial subject. Exploring the co-production of race, space, and the racial subject enables an analysis of how the City of Toronto may both enact and react to racialized difference, in local and site-specific ways.

Methodology

Sara Ahmed (2012) calls for a genealogy of the term "diversity" in order to better understand its institutional appeal, as well as for us "to have conversations with each other from our specific locations" (p. 16) to understand how diversity manifests in the local. In this paper, I draw on a genealogical framework to explicate the historical, political, social, and cultural "truths" of diversity discourse in the City of Toronto, as well as how and under what conditions they are reproduced in the space of the City of Toronto. I seek to unravel what appears as self-evident and linear, to show the discontinuities, exclusions, and alternative accounts of diversity in the City of Toronto so that its perceived essence and logic can be situated within a larger political, economic, and racial project.

Foucault (1984) believed that genealogy conveyed how truth and its effects could not be separated from its processes of production.

Thus, through genealogy one could draw attention to the illegitimate, disqualified knowledges of a discourse against what was taken to be its 'truths,' in order to expose the processes of the production of knowledge as *political processes* (Foucault, 1980). Using a genealogical framework, I began to explore the productive and political workings of truth and power by unearthing the "local, discontinuous, disqualified, illegitimate knowledges" (Foucault, 1980, p. 83) of diversity discourse in the City of Toronto. In the following pages, I draw on examples from a textual analysis I conducted on Committee and Council documents of the City of Toronto from 1980 to the present which named and/or offered policy directions on race, racism, and/or diversity, in order to observe and trace the multiple and contradictory political moments which make up diversity.[3] I refer to these City documents as "texts" because, following Dorothy Smith (1999), texts become "active" through their reading by coordinating the activities of many to (re-)produce certain social, historical, and material relations (p. 135). Although the diverse object and subject appear in City texts as having a point of origin and inner meaning in history, the goal of this paper is to begin to unearth how diversity in the City of Toronto accumulates into a series of events, bending to the will of political and racial forces and their effects.

---

3   This textual analysis was conducted as part of my doctoral dissertation research. The themes and analyses that I include in this paper were considered as possible chapters of my dissertation, but were parsed out due to limitations of space/pages. The documents included in this paper were selected from a list of hundreds of policy documents which named either "race," "racism" and/or "diversity", and then when a deeper investigation was required due to the absence of electronic databasing and/or loss of paper indexing, search terms were extended (some on the advice of City of Toronto Archives Staff) to "race," "race relations," "anti-racism," "multicultural," "diversity management," "equity," "human rights," "Employment Equity Act," "Employee and Labour Relations," and "Aboriginal". These texts which were grouped into several themes, including "the Good Sell" and "Invitation to Encounter," which were not included in my dissertation.

Diversity Exposed

Ahmed (2012) draws on Fanon to emphasize how bodies become racialized through encounters. For example, racialization was crucial to the imperial project, whereby white and black bodies *were produced* as ontologically and epistemologically different through civil/uncivil, moral/immoral, and clean/impure dichotomies, in order to justify colonial violence. Ahmed (2012) also argues that "race is an *effect* of racialization" (p. 47); the meanings and "essences" attached to racial bodies through racialization are incited into discourses of race, and reified through the white masculine subject's field of knowledge which desires to impart the "truth" about the racial Other.

Following Ahmed, I contend that diversity discourse reproduces and (re-)organizes race in the City of Toronto through racialization and the re-making of the racial subject. Using examples from City of Toronto texts, I also show how the construction of spatially bound innocence (the denial of racism in space) is co-constituted with the repetition of racialization which attempts to fix the encountered racial Other in space. In City texts, any references to race or racism, as embodied or experienced (i.e. barriers to access, human rights violations or hate crimes based on race) are reframed and folded into a pre-existing "diversity" agenda which occludes and/or erases experiences of racism via reifying and organizing the space and bodies of the City in colonial and racial terms. As Claudia Matus and Marta Infante (2011) write:

> The construction of diversity requires a counterpart: discrimination. This, if unproblematized, legitimates the oppositional resistance to 'diversity'. Thus, it is 'natural' to engage in discriminatory practices…but what is not at stake are those who are dictating the norms about who will be penalized and for what differences. (Matus and Infante, 2011, p. 304)

I want to build on Matus and Infante's idea that discrimination is normalized in the construction of diversity to suggest that the reproduction of racialization and race is precisely what makes diversity in the City of Toronto thrive. I argue that diversity in the City of Toronto requires and *normalizes* racialization in order to be able to co-articulate racial difference and spatial innocence. It is through this co-articulation, which draws upon and recites racial logics and truths, that the reproduction of the historical, ontological, political, and economic violence of race in the City of Toronto is made possible. In other words, racialization essentializes and organizes racial Others in order to make up the "difference" of diversity, at the same time that experiences of race/racism are repeatedly occluded or erased in order to reproduce the City of Toronto as a leader in managing (read: knowing) "them" *and* as a space of innocence.

Here I also want to challenge Ahmed's (2012) conceptualization of commitments to diversity as non-performative. Ahmed builds on Butler's (1993) theorization of non-performativity, which requires that discourse *does not* "produce the effects that it names" (p. 2), to argue that "the failure of a speech act to do what it says....is actually *what the speech act is doing*" (Ahmed, 2012, p. 117). For Ahmed, to name is a way to not bring something into effect; the saying stands in for the *not doing*. I want to complicate her theorizing of non-performativity to suggest that what diversity in the City of Toronto names and/or says is premised on and reproduces racial terms, and therefore that the "saying" of diversity discourse cannot be separated from what it *does*. If race is an effect of racialization, as Ahmed suggests, and diversity discourse invites and reproduces race via racialization, how can what diversity names be separated from its norms and modes of production/ re-articulation, even in what it promises to be and *do*? I want to use the idea of ethnic harmony in the City as an example of diversity as a performative. Does the naming of the City as an ethnically harmonious space via diversity discourse not require racialization and race, as well as their reproductions, as effects of its naming *and* doing? Similarly, does the naming of the City as a leader in managing diversity not require the reproduction and effects of racialization as well, whether occluded or rendered partially visible, as "cultural difference"? I ask: Is diversity in the City of Toronto really non-performative if, as a reiterative practice which conceals the racial norms that are incited into and reproduced by it, diversity does what it intends precisely through what it names/ says? In the following pages, I organize my analyses around two themes, diversity as the "good sell" and diversity as invitation to encounter, to show how diversity discourse in the City of Toronto is a performative. I trace how the re-citing of diversity incites and reproduces racializing ideas and practices, which occlude the existence of racism in order to name the City as a space of leadership and innocence.

Diversity as the "Good Sell"

"TORONTO THE DIVERSE"

- ▶ Multiple ethnic cultures: 160 countries
- ▶ 1-of-3 GTA residents is a visible minority
- ▶ Religious freedom
- ▶ Inclusive
- ▶ A City of nations (Chinatown, etc.)
- ▶ Caribana: largest West Indian event in North America
    ("Increasing Toronto's profile internationally and at home (all wards)", City of Toronto, 2002a, p. 12)

Yasmeen Abu-Laban and Christina Gabriel (2002) write about the intrinsic value and broader trend of "'selling diversity' – whereby the skills, talents, and ethnic backgrounds of men and women are commodified, marketed, and billed as trade-enhancing" in Canada (p. 12). Catungal and Leslie (2009) and Shaw (2007) further assert that diversity is a consumable product of whiteness. Only those who have the class, cash, and right ethnicity can enjoy the rewards and benefits of "ethnic" diversity (Shaw, 2007, p. 95). Diversity draws directly on corporate logic, market based strategies, and the achievement of goals and standards alongside the management and containment of internal differences.

Diversity as a concept and as a discourse is used frequently by the city of Toronto to promote a strong economy and to attract tourism, investment, and capital. For example, in 2002, the City of Toronto embarked on three-year marketing plan with a "branding strategy" in order to increase its profile internationally and at home, and to increase its global competitiveness (City of Toronto, 2002a). As part of the plan, the City sought to highlight Toronto's "ethnocultural diversity as one of its major competitive advantages and community strengths" (International Policy Framework for the City of Toronto, 2002b, p.4), and includes the following statement from the Toronto Economic Development Strategy, approved in 2000 by Toronto City Council:

> Nowhere else in the world do so many people from so many different cultures, different ethnic background, different religions, races, creeds, color, sexual orientation, live together in peace, harmony, and mutual respect (City of Toronto, 2002a, p. 2).

The City's $500k branding strategy, developed in consultation with five City departments and external consultants, included the theme "Toronto The Diverse," which seeks to promote the city as a space that is "inclusive" and where there is "religious freedom," to name a few (City of Toronto, 2002a, p. 12).

However, during the same year that the branding strategy was developed and put forward to Toronto City Council, a Toronto Response for Youth (TRY) program was being developed in response to concerns of "a significant increase in the number of incidents of hate and racism directed against members of Toronto's Muslim communities following the attacks in the United States on September 11, 2001" (p. 1), and "crime statistics released in the spring of 2002 by the Toronto Police Service which revealed that hate crimes against Muslims in Toronto had more than doubled" (City of Toronto, 2002c, p. 2). Earlier that same year, a Notice of Motion was also put forward concerning the vandalism of the Gayatri Mandir, a Hindu Temple in Toronto, which included the following statements:

WHEREAS Toronto City Council has taken a leadership role to respect and to celebrate the diversity among the people of Toronto; and

WHEREAS Toronto City Council has adopted many policies and programs which respect our diversity; and

WHEREAS on February 8, 2002, the Gayatri Mandir at Dupont Street and Ossington Avenue in the City of Toronto was vandalized...

NOW THEREFORE BE IT RESOLVED THAT City Council express its distress, deepest concern and indignation about these hate crimes and join with the Federation of Hindu Temples of Canada in condemning these acts... (City of Toronto, 2002d, p. 31).

In 2003, a report and subsequent Notice of Motion was issued concerning the "60.48 percent increase in anti-Semitic incidents in 2002...the highest number recorded in the 20-year history" (City of Toronto, 2003b, p. 17). The Notice of Motion included the statement that because "anti-Semitism is incompatible with Toronto's slogan: 'Diversity is our Strength,'" Toronto City Council should pass a resolution "strongly condemning all acts of anti-Semitism and all forms of racism" (City of Toronto, 2003b, p. 17).

bell hooks (1992) writes how the Other, encountered in politically progressive spaces, must assume "recognizable forms"; where voices of non-white Others are first enabled, and then "eaten, consumed, and forgotten" (p. 26). In the texts noted above, the City of Toronto repeatedly marketing itself internationally and locally as being "good at" and/or a leader in diversity enables and is enabled by the racialization and commodification of its "diverse" populations, premised on the evocation and occlusion/erasure of experiences of racism in the City. I argue that racialized Others and their experiences of racism become recognizable, and that they become *subjects* in the City, only in their consumed, de-contextualized, and re-branded forms. This subjectivity is premised on the reproduction of essentialist representations of the non-white Other, as co-constructed with the occlusion and/or denial of (their) experiences of racism in the City, which directly informs and is informed by how the City is good at and/or a leader in diversity. What I am suggesting here is that experiences of racism in the diverse City become *necessary*; that they are deliberately evoked as signs of racial difference which are then re-framed/commodified and erased once they, and the bodies that have been subjected to them *and by them*, have been "eaten". The processes of evocation, consumption, and reframing are precisely the moments where race is reproduced *through racialization*, where Othered bodies serve a particular cultural and consumable fantasy of Otherness in the diverse City, and as a reconfirmation of whiteness and power.

The City also markets itself as a "global city" where immigrants are welcomed and are an integral part of the celebrated cultural diversity and economic viability that makes up Toronto's unique character. For example, in a request to Toronto City Council to cover additional expenses of hosting the 2005 Metropolis Congress, the benefits of hosting included showcasing how the City, "as one of the most ethno-racially diverse cities in the world, can demonstrate how it has successfully integrated newcomers into the fabric of Canadian society," and how it can "boost Toronto's international image as a leader in dealing with immigration and settlement issues," who is willing to share their experiences and successes with other cities (City of Toronto, 2004, p. 5). Similarly, in the City of Toronto's 2006 Creative City Report, which seeks to highlight Toronto's creative and growing cultural sector in order to position the city internationally and to attract local and regional investment, Toronto's immigrant populations are conveyed as a source of creative talent and economic growth, where they "bring their skills, experience, social network, and artistic traditions to the city," but also as evidence of the City's inclusive nature: "their very presence stands as an indicator of the city's openness to diverse newcomers" (City of Toronto, 2006, p. 19).

However, in City texts, the existence of racism does not entirely disappear. In 2002, the "City of Toronto Immigration and Settlement Communications Framework" outlines the need to translate key City materials into various languages, to increase outreach through ethnic media, and to increase the presence of multilingual staff in order for newcomers to have increased access to City services. Indicated very briefly in the report is that the communications framework must also support the removal of *"systemic barriers such as racism and the lack of recognition of overseas education, qualifications, or work experience"* (2002e, p. 6; my emphasis). This statement is immediately followed by an understanding that information in languages from the most frequent countries of immigrant origin is vastly required, as it further enables the City to respond to immigration and settlement issues, and to encourage a positive climate and attitude towards newcomers that the City is known for. Similarly, the City of Toronto Plan of Action for the Elimination of Racism and Discrimination (City of Toronto, 2003) begins with the claim that "Toronto is one of the most diverse cities in the world and has gained an international reputation for the successful *management of its diversity*" (City of Toronto, 2003, p. 2; my emphasis), and that the Plan is but one of the ways in which "the City of Toronto continues its leadership role in building a society that respects and values the diversity among the peoples of the City of Toronto" (p. 3). The 2000 Ornstein study, the City-commissioned study on ethno-racial inequality in Toronto which sparked the Plan, concluded that for ethno-racial minorities with similar education, the levels of unemployment and poverty are significantly higher than for persons of European origin. The City of Toronto Plan identifies these labor market and economic disparities that may be experienced by racialized and/or immigrant communities *due to racism*, and suggests:

> integrating into the City's labour force development plans co-operative strategies to address unique needs of diverse communities to ameliorate labour market and economic disparities, *implement mentoring programs* to assist employees and immigrant workers,

continue outreach and information initiatives so that businesses from diverse communities have access to the procurement process of the City and agencies. (City of Toronto, 2003, p. 6; my emphasis)

Himani Bannerji (2000) argues that as an ideological tool, diversity re-packages un- or underemployment into issues of culture rather than as evidence of racism. I want to build on Bannerji's analysis to offer that the City's continued leadership in the area of diversity is co-constructed with racializing practices which are premised on the essentialized inferiority of racialized bodies. The discourse of diversity re-circulates racializing norms by suggesting that issues of racism and/or unemployment of racialized Others in the City can be resolved by translation and mentoring; which identifies "their" *lack* of knowledge and language skills in order to conceal and continue to deny racism (and accountability for racism) in the space of the City. The denial of racism in the space of the City, which keeps the City of Toronto's local and world leader status intact, is thus premised on the reproduction of racialization and racial thinking which is incited into and incited by diversity discourse in the City of Toronto.

Reframing experiences of racism in the City as difficulties experienced due to language barriers and/or lack of skills, knowledge, training and/or education is prominent in and across several City of Toronto diversity texts, dating as far back as the 1980s. What becomes interesting here is the extent to which the City re-circulates the embodiment of lack (of language, knowledge, and/or skills), in order to re-frame and/or deny the existence of racism, and to reassert itself as a leader in issues of diversity. For example, the "Deputy Mayor's Black Business Professionals Roundtable" report (City of Toronto, 2014) suggests that issues faced by Black business owners and operators in the City could be resolved by "building education and awareness," "skills development workshops," and "creating a business professionals mentorship program" for the Black business community (p. 10). Experiences of racism were mentioned nowhere in the report. The report also includes a note from Toronto City Councilor Michael Thompson, which states:

> Diversity is Toronto's strength … what we learned and shared at the Black Business Professionals Roundtable will go a long way toward building productive ongoing collaboration and instituting effective support services (City of Toronto, 2014a, p. iii).

In response to the escalating hate crimes against Muslim groups in Toronto in 2002, the City of Toronto created a youth *mentoring program* (TRY), which recruits and trains "at-risk youth" to become peer leaders to assist other young people in dealing with issues related to Islamophobia and other forms of racism, but to also provide at-risk racialized youth with "employment and life skills" (City of Toronto, 2002c, p. 2), in order to gain long-term employment. The report also notes that the TRY project "has the potential to be a useful model for other communities," given that it is a "unique City-run project which has been built on a foundation of community partnerships" (p. 3). Through the re-circulation of translation services, mentoring, training and skills development, the City perpetually links barriers to access, employment and/or experiences of racism in the City with "their" (racialized Others') lack of skills, knowledge, education, language, and/or training. This deliberate linking of the reproduction of racialization and the erasure of racism enables a re-citing of the City's claims of leadership and innocence. In other words, the more translation services and mentoring are repeated in City texts, the more the shift from racism to racialization, the more innocent the City space, the more successful the City of Toronto becomes at being a leader in "managing" diversity via addressing "their" *lack*.

The City's Human Resources Action Plan on Access, Equity, and Human Rights 2007– 2008 lists several initiatives for the City to *continue* to achieve diversity and inclusiveness in the Toronto Public Service, including to strengthen relationships with the Aboriginal community, but also "to increase understanding of managers regarding their obligations under the Ontario Human Rights Code and to prevent and eliminate racism and racial barriers in the TPS" (City of Toronto, 2008, p. 5). In the Plan, a Mentoring program that assists Black African Canadian employees is listed as an initiative which is "effective in addressing issues of *systemic discrimination,*" particularly the underrepresentation of Black African Canadian senior employees in the City; yet the program is also listed as beneficial for City staff who "learn mentoring and coaching skills and increase their understanding of *cross-cultural issues*" (p. 9; my emphases). The elimination of racial barriers and racism in the City again becomes coupled with the mentoring of Black African Canadians, whereby their lack of knowledge and skills becomes the reason for their lack of access and mobility in the City. However, the existence of racism becomes re-framed as *distinctly cultural issues* which "City staff" (read: white) can learn about in order to *manage.* Page 12 of the Plan also notes that the City won several awards for participation in this Mentoring program in 2007.[4]

---

4   Other examples include the "1986-1990 Equal Opportunity Program Review" report which outlines how racialized and Native employees are significantly underrepresented in the City and "have historically faced systemic barriers to employment" (p. 69). The report suggests "internship/bridging/apprenticeship positions" and training strategies to give employees "the knowledge, skills, and experience to compete successfully" (p. 70). In May of 1991, the City of Toronto created the "Multicultural Access Program" (MAP) in response to problems that members of ethnic and racial minorities had encountered in getting access to municipal services (City of Toronto, 1990). Consultations with racial and ethnic groups began as early as 1984, but particular emphasis was placed on inviting new immigrants who, *because of their cultural and language backgrounds*, had difficulty in getting adequate access to services (City of Toronto, 1990, p. 152; my emphasis). Even though racism and discrimination were identified in the consultations as a core issue in terms of accessing service, the City's response was to "provide better information on City services in a variety of languages and media" (City of Toronto, 1992, p. 120).

In this section of the paper, I have shown how the City of Toronto's marketing of itself as being "good at" and/or a local and world leader in diversity is directly linked with reproducing racialization and race, which simultaneously occludes and/or denies the existence of racism in the space of the City. The City's leadership on managing diversity is repeated in and across several City texts, but what becomes concealed is how the City co-constructs this leadership with the re-circulation of racial norms that reinscribes racialization of the Other, in order to disavow the racist and racializing practices that would threaten its local and international leadership status. Through re-significations of racial difference and the normalization of (racial) lack, which are incited into and incited by the discourse of diversity, race simultaneously flourishes and is concealed in the City.

Building upon my earlier argument that diversity discourse in the City of Toronto is performative, I also want to suggest that the City marketing itself as "inclusive," as a space of "religious freedom," and as a leader in diversity can only be accomplished via the commodification of racial subjects. What diversity names and the effects it produces are both made possible through the reproduction of racialization and race, and as such, the saying/naming cannot be separated from the *doing* of diversity. In the next section of this paper, I discuss further how the reproduction of racialization and race are inextricably linked to the performativity of diversity discourse and the simultaneous occlusion/denial of racism in the space of the City, through exploring the invitation to racial Others into consultations in the City of Toronto.

Diversity as Invitation to Encounter

Participants expressed frustration that they were being consulted again. Individuals and community groups asked why they were being consulted when the City and other governments had a catalogue of actions that could be taken.

("City of Toronto Plan of Action for the
Elimination of Racism and Discrimination",
City of Toronto, 2003a, p. 27)

They [participants] welcomed the opportunity to
participate in these consultations with one of the few
orders of government where discussion on issues of
diversity is taking place. Participants expressed hope
that the City of Toronto would continue to act as an
advocate on behalf of its residents despite the current
political climate, and that the City would continue to
lead the country in addressing issues of diversity.

("City of Toronto Plan of Action for the
Elimination of Racism and Discrimination",
City of Toronto, 2003a, p. 28)

In her book *Woman, Native, Other*, Min-Ha Trinh (1989) suggests that
the invitation to the "native Other" to contribute their voice in dominant
systems and hierarchies re-ignites the "us" and "them" dichotomy that
rationalizes socio-racial and spatial relations of power. In this practice,
the native Other is both taken up as the "voice of truth" and re-written
by the white male in his own language, to reproduce and manage racial
demarcations (1989, p. 67). The co-construction of the occlusion/denial
of experiences of racism with the reproduction of racialization and race
is evident in and across several City of Toronto texts which discuss the
invitation to racial Others to be "consulted" on how to address issues of
racism. For example, to prepare for the City of Toronto's Plan of Action
for the Elimination of Racism and Discrimination (City of Toronto,
2003a), approximately 50 community consultation sessions were held,
where over 1,000 people participated and contributed their thoughts
on how the City could combat increasing experiences of racism and
discrimination in Toronto. In the appended summary notes of the
consultations were several statements about experiences of racism in the
city, and of the need for the City to be held accountable in addressing
racism:

Since 9/11, Muslim is a euphemism for walking bomb.
Racism is a growing problem in Toronto. How do I
know? I know because the number of attacks on me
keeps increasing.
There is no safe place. (City of Toronto, 2003a, p. 29)

However, in the body of the Plan, the City is again reproduced as a leader
in managing issues of diversity via the occlusion/erasure of experiences
of racism. Included in the Plan of Action report is a statement of how
the invitation to residents, community groups, and organizations to
give their input on the Plan of Action is an example of how the City
"build(s) on the legacy and leadership for which the City is known"(City
of Toronto, 2003a, p. 25). The report also closes with the following:

Diversity is a fundamental characteristic of our city.
It gives Toronto strength through an ability to value,
celebrate and respect differences. It is this recognition
of diversity, which makes Toronto one of the most
creative, caring and successful cities in the world (City
of Toronto, 2003a, p. 20).

There is a certain irony attached to the statement that diversity makes
Toronto one of the most caring cities in the world in a report which
seeks to eliminate racism and discrimination. Those who feel that
being Muslim is equated with a walking bomb, those who experience
increasing racial attacks, and those who never feel safe, would hardly
call the city they live in a place that celebrates and respects differences.
Furthermore, participants' frustrations at being consulted become re-
framed in the Plan of Action in order to demonstrate the City's leadership
on diversity, as well as their democratic nature. Consultations which
were originally frustrating become yet another welcomed opportunity
for "diverse" communities to participate, which the City then links to
its proactive stance in *inviting and leading* discussions of diversity.

Ahmed (2012) explains that in institutions that embrace diversity, "moments of complaint" (i.e. discussions of race/racism) become opportunities to promote the values of diversity, which prevents messages about racism from being heard (p. 145). Trinh (1989) also aptly writes that the invitation to sit at the table with "us" appropriates and reduces "them" to a detached "us" discourse. The invitation evokes a grateful witness who mimics and legalizes the discourse. A "them" among "us" is thus "a hoax; a false incorporation that leaves 'them' barer than ever, if 'them' allows itself to nibble at the bait of Lies" (Trinh, 1989, p. 67). I want to expand Ahmed and Trinh, particularly their conceptualizations of the failure to hear about racism and the invitation into mimicry, to include an understanding of diversity discourse as a hailing, whereby racial Others come to know themselves and be known as *subjects* through the discourse of diversity. Diversity discourse draws out (hails) repeated consultations with racial Others under the guise of addressing experiences of racism in the City, however what becomes concealed is how the racial Others who participate in consultation processes are both regulated and reproduced through diversity discourse, *as racialized subjects*, via the continued re-framing of their experiences. For example, in 1991, the Toronto Mayor's Committee on Community and Race Relations held a public meeting, given the poor relations between the Black community and Toronto Police Service (TPS), "to hear from all spectrums of the Black Community about those relations and to avail the Black Community of an opportunity to express those concerns and give the Committee input on changes to the Police Act" (City of Toronto, 1991, p. 204). The meeting, which in the end recommended further "private meetings between the Mayor, some members of the Committee, and the Black Community, to restore mutual respect and trust between the Black Community and the police" (p. 204) was included in a report for the 1991 program and budget of the Committee, in order to demonstrate the importance of celebrating *diversity* in the City of Toronto, and in particular to request for additional funds to celebrate Black History Month.

In the City of Toronto, experiences of racism become re-framed via the continued consultation and participation of racial Others, which I argue both authorize and are hailed by diversity discourse. I also argue that the establishment of these consultations, particularly what they come to represent in terms of achieving "democratic participation" and commitments to address marginalization/racism in the City, are repetitive and idealized *performances* of diversity, as a set of practices which acquire value and meaning through the reproduction and occlusion of race/racialization in the City. Although the City might also repeat its claims of successfully addressing racism in the City and achieving democratic participation in order to disguise that they can never finally or fully be addressed or achieved, I again want to suggest, following my earlier argument on the performativity of diversity discourse, that the saying/naming of success and achievement and the doing of it both require and reproduce racialization and race.

Another example of consultation and the hailing of racial subjects is the response to the 2002 Council Motion on Racial Profiling in Toronto, which references reports over three decades on racial profiling of the Black community in Toronto. Police Chief Julian Fantino "met with members of the Black community" and made commitments, following these consultations, to "enhance the TPS recruit orientation and training programs by arranging face to face meetings with police recruits and members of the Black community prior to their graduation," and to coordinate a "Race Relations Conference" in Toronto where the TPS, the Black community and all levels of civil society/government focus on problem solving" (City of Toronto, 2003c, p.7). Furthermore, the City's Race and Ethnic Relations Committee writes in the same report that "sufficient studies and reports have been prepared on the subject of racial profiling and systemic racism over the last 27 years," and, based on the recommendations of these various reports, believes that it is *"now time for action on this important matter"* (City of Toronto, 2003c, p. 21; my emphasis). The action that the City's Race and Ethnic Relations Committee recommends is for groups such as the African Legal Clinic, Toronto Police Services Board, and other stakeholders to be invited to make deputations to the January 23, 2003 meeting of City Council. What I am suggesting here is that the practice of inviting, meeting, and consulting with racialized Others in order to address issues of racism in the City reproduces claims of City's leadership on issues of diversity, precisely because of what these consultations accomplish: the repeated occlusion/writing out of experiences of racism in the City via the reproduction of racialization and race. It is also through consultation that accountability for racism in the space of the City *by the City* is erased.

In Judith Butler's (2011) description and analyses of performativity, she writes that "the ideal that is mirrored depends on that very mirroring to be sustained as an ideal" (p. xxiii). In the City of Toronto, consultations with "the community" (i.e. residents of Toronto, community groups, and agencies) are prioritized and idealized because they reflect and entrench the idea of democratic political participation; one in which everyone has an equal voice, and the right to speak.[5] However, in the City of Toronto, diversity discourse draws racialized Others into consultation processes in order to reproduce the encounter, whereby racializing norms are repeated and attached to racial Others/subjects in order to occlude or deny the existence of racism in the City. Furthermore, the continued invitation, presence, and/or participation of racialized Others in the City

---

5   See for example the "International Policy Framework for the City of Toronto" which states "The City of Toronto is a leader in developing innovative policies dealing with the issues of ethno-racial diversity and equity...The Task Force Report sets out major principles of access, transparency, participation and inclusive decision-making processes... The City of Toronto strives to actively engage its citizenry, especially marginalized groups, in the policy development process" (City of Toronto, 2002, p. 12). Similarly, the City's "Status Report - Implementation of 2004-2006 Access, Equity and Human Rights Action Plans" which states, "active involvement by Toronto's diverse communities is in line with the trend for enhanced local democracy and public accountability and opening up the process of local government so that residents can influence decision-making in the City"(City of Toronto, 2006, p.3).

is in itself seen as antiracist *action*, in spite of or, as I argue, *because of* how the presence of racialized Others is taken up and commodified in the diverse City, to mean the City's leadership on democratic participation. What becomes concealed by and through the repeated invitations to consult is how racism in the City actually gets addressed. I want to again suggest here that the encounter with racial Others and the invitation to discuss their experiences of racism are *necessary* to the reproduction of racialization and race, the re-constitution and performativity of diversity discourse, and to the City of Toronto's status as a leader on issues of diversity and democracy.

Some Final Thoughts

Ahmed (2007) and Shaw (2007) argue that the elusive nature and lack of clear definition of diversity is exactly what allows the term to signify the inclusion *and* exclusion, transcendence *and* containment of racialized bodies. Expanding on Judith Butler's (2011) theorization of performativity, I have shown how the racial norms that are incited into diversity discourse in the City of Toronto are reproduced through the commodification of Otherness and occlusion of experiences of racism in the City. In this paper, I have also begun to make visible the regulatory, racial norms that are "indissociable" (Butler, 2011, p. xiii) from the materialization of diverse (raced) bodies, texts, and speech acts. Diversity discourse in the City of Toronto thus becomes performative by drawing on and re-circulating historical and racial norms to make racial Others intelligible, as *subjects*, through speech acts and through texts, via processes of racialization.

Louise Archer (2007) writes about how through its emotive appeal, diversity re-frames and renders unintelligible any efforts to expose racism, because they are seen to be threatening to the progressive and democratic nature of Toronto, and by extension to its tolerant and welcoming citizenry. In this paper, I have extended Archer's analysis to argue that diversity is simultaneously racialized and *spatialized*. As I have shown, diversity discourse in the City of Toronto is made possible through the reinscription of racialization and the re-making of the racial subject, in order to reproduce and mark the City of Toronto as a diverse space where racism does not, *and cannot*, penetrate. Spatial innocence is thus collapsed with the reproduction of racialization, race, and racial subject. Diversity discourse sets the stage in which the spatial denial of racism not only attempts to foreclose any agency on the part of the Other, it also justifies the City of Toronto's repeated colonial and racializing interventions under the guise of eliminating racism: a racism that becomes intelligible only to incite future interventions in diversity's name.

References

Abu-Laban, Y. & Gabriel, C. (2002). *Selling diversity: Immigration, multiculturalism, employment equity, and globalization*. Toronto: Broadview Press.

Ahmed, S. (2000). *Strange encounters: Embodied others in post-coloniality*. London and New York: Routledge.

Ahmed, S. (2006). The non-performativity of anti-racism. *Meridians, 7*(1), 104-126.

Ahmed, S. (2007). The language of diversity. *Ethnic and Racial Studies, 30*(2), 235-256.

Ahmed, S. (2012). *On being included: Racism and diversity ininstitutional life*. London, UK: Duke University Press.

Altilia, C. (2003). Planning for diversity in the global city: The Toronto case. Retrieved from

http://www.yorku.ca/fes/research/docs/carol_altilia.pdf

Archer, L. (2007). Diversity, equality, and higher education: A critical reflection on the ab/uses of equity discourse within widening participation. *Teaching in Higher Education, 12*(5-6), 635-653.

Arrington, C.E. & Francis, J.R. (1989). Letting the chat out of the bag: Deconstruction, privilege and accounting research. *Accounting, Organizations and Society,* 14(1/2), 1-28.

Bannerji, H. (2000). The paradox of diversity: The construction of a multicultural Canada and "women of colour". *Women's Studies International Forum, 23,* (5), 537-560.

Boudreau, J., Keil, R. &Young, D. (2009). *Changing Toronto: Governing urban neoliberalism.* Toronto: University of Toronto Press.

Butler, J. (2011). *Bodies that matter: On the discursive limits of sex.* New York: Routledge.

Catungal, J. P. & Leslie, D. (2009).Contesting the creative city: Race, nation, multiculturalism. *Geoforum, 40,* 701-704.

City of Toronto (1991). *Executive Committee Report No. 1 for City Council Consideration at Meeting No. 2 on January 15, 1991. Clause 45 – Toronto Mayor's Committee on Community and Race Relations – 1991 Program and Budget* (p. 203-205).

City of Toronto (2002a). *Increasing Toronto's profile internationally and at home (all wards).*Retrieved from http://www.toronto.ca/legdocs/2002/agendas/council/cc021126/edp10rpt/cl001.pdf

City of Toronto (2002b). *International policy framework for the City of Toronto.* Retrieved from http://www.toronto.ca/legdocs/2002/agendas/council/cc020521/pof8rpt/cl009.pdf

City of Toronto (2002c). *Update on Toronto response for youth (TRY).* Retrieved from http://www.toronto.ca/legdocs/2002/agendas/committees/cms/cms020624/it015.pdf

City of Toronto (2002d). *Certificate of amendments: (5) Vandalism of the Gayatri Mandir* (p. 31). Retrieved from http://www.toronto.ca/ legdocs/2002/agendas/council/cc020304/cofa.pdf

City of Toronto (2002e). *Toronto immigration and settlement communications framework.* Retrieved from http://www.toronto.ca/ legdocs/2002/agendas/council/cc021029/cms9rpt/cl001.pdf

City of Toronto (2003a).*City of Toronto plan of action for the elimination of racism and discrimination.* Retrieved from http://www.toronto.ca/ legdocs/2003/agendas/council/cc030414/pof3rpt/cl003.pdf

City of Toronto (2003b). *Policy and finance committee agenda: (19) Rise in hate incidents for the year 2002* (p. 17). Retrieved from http://www. toronto.ca/legdocs/2003/agendas/committees/pof/pof030710/agenda. pdf

City of Toronto (2003c). *Update – Council motion on racial profiling in Toronto.* Retrieved from http://www.toronto.ca/legdocs/2003/agendas/ council/cc030204/pof1rpt/cl016.pdf

City of Toronto (2004). *Hosting the 2005 metropolis congress in Toronto.* Retrieved from

http://www.toronto.ca/legdocs/2004/agendas/committees/bu/ bud040324/it005a.pdf

City of Toronto (2006). *Strategies for a creative city report (all wards).* Retrieved from http://www.toronto.ca/legdocs/2006/agendas/ committees/edp/edp060912/it018.pdf

City of Toronto (2008). *Appendix: Reporting to Shirley Hoy. Access, equity and human rights action plan part 1 - 2007-2008.* Retrieved from http:// www.toronto.ca/legdocs/mmis/2008/ex/bgrd/backgroundfile-13970. pdf

Clayton, J. (2008). Everyday geographies of marginality and encounter in the multicultural city. In C. Dwyer & C. Bressey (Eds.), *New geographies of race and racism* (pp. 255-268). Burlington, VT: Ashgate Publishing Company.

Cross, M. & Keith, M. (1993). Racism and the postmodern city. In M. Cross & M. Keith (Eds.), *Racism, the city and the state* (pp. 1-30). New York: Routledge.

Croucher, S. L. (1997). Constructing the image of ethnic harmony in Toronto Canada: The politics of problem definition and nondefinition. *Urban Affairs Review,* 32 (3), 319-347.

Foucault, M. (1980). Two lectures. In C. Gordon (Ed.), *Power/ Knowledge: Selected interviews and other writings 1972-1977* (pp. 78-108). New York, NY: Pantheon.

Foucault, M. (1984). Truth and power. In P. Rabinow (Ed.), *The Foucault reader* (pp. 51-75). New York: Random House Inc.

Good, K. R. (2009). *Municipalities and multiculturalism - The politics of immigration in Toronto and Vancouver.* Toronto: University of Toronto Press.

Goonewardena, K. & Kipfer, S. (2005). Spaces of difference: Reflections from Toronto on multiculturalism, bourgeois urbanism and the possibility of radical urban politics. *International Journal of Urban and Regional Research, 29*(3).

hooks, b. (1992). *Black looks: Race and representation* (pp. 21-40). Boston, MA: South End Press.

Isin, E. & Siemiatycki, M. (1997). Immigration, Diversity and Urban Citizenship in Toronto. *Canadian Journal of Regional Science, 21*(2), 73–102.

Jacobs, J.M. (1996). *The edge of empire: Postcolonialism and the city.* New York: Routledge.

Jordan, G. & Weedon, C. (2015). The celebration of difference and the cultural politics of racism. In B. Adam & S. Allan (Eds.), *Theorizing culture: An interdisciplinary critique after postmodernism* (pp. 149-164). New York: Routledge.

Keith, M. (2002). The mirage at the heart of the myth? Thinking about the white city. In D. T. Goldberg & J. Solomos (Eds.), *A companion to racial and ethnic studies* (pp. 323-339). Massachusetts, MA: Blackwell Publishing.

Kipfer, S. (2007). Fanon and space: Colonization, urbanization, and liberation from the colonial to the global city. *Environment and Planning D: Society and Space, 25,* 701-726.

Kirova, A. (2008). Critical and emerging discourses in multicultural education literature: A review. *Canadian Ethnic Studies, 40,* 1-2, 101-124.

Kymlicka, W. (1995). *Multicultural citizenship: A liberal theory of minority rights.* Oxford: Oxford University Press.

Kymlicka, W. & Banting, K. (2006). Introduction: Multiculturalism and the welfare state. In W. Kymlicka & L. Banting (Eds.), *Multiculturalism and the welfare state: Recognition and redistribution in contemporary democracies.* Oxford: Oxford University Press.

Matus, C. & Infante, M. (2011). Undoing diversity: Knowledge and neoliberal discourses in colleges of education. *Discourse: Studies in the Cultural Politics of Education, 32* (3), 293-307.

Nagle, J. (2009). *Multiculturalism's double-bind: Creating inclusivity, cosmopolitanism and difference.* Burlington, VT: Ashgrave Publishing Company.

Ornstein, M. (2000). *Ethno-racial inequality in the city of Toronto: An analysis of the 1996 census.* Retrieved from http://tobiashouse.ca/passport/profiles/pdf/EthnoRacial_Inequality.pdf

Parekh, B. (2006). *Rethinking multiculturalism: Cultural diversity and political theory* (2nd ed.). London, UK: Palgrave.

Puwar, N. (2004). Space invaders: Race, gender and bodies out of place. Oxford and New York: Berg Publishers.

Saloojee, A. & Siemiatycki, M. (2002). Ethnoracial political representation in Toronto: Patterns and problems. Journal of International Migration and Integration, *3*(2), 241-273.

Shaw, W. S. (2007). *Cities of whiteness.* Oxford, UK: Blackwell Publishing.

Smith, M. (2010). Gender, whiteness and "other Others" in the academy. In S. Razack, S. Thobani & M. Smith (Eds.), *States of race: Critical race feminism for the 21st century.* Toronto: Between the Lines.

Stoler, A. L. (1995). *Race and the education of desire: Foucault's history of sexuality and the colonial order of things.* London, UK: Duke University Press.

Trinh, M. (1989). *Woman, native, other.* Indianapolis, IN: Indiana University Press.

SIX

CONTEXTUALIZING DIVERSITY'S (NON-)PERFORMATIVITY

Eike Marten
FernUniversität in Hagen

Correspondence: Eike Marten, FernUniversität in Hagen[1]
eike.marten@fernuni-hagen.de

Abstract

The article contextualizes the traveled skeptical evaluation of diversity as a 'non-performative' (Ahmed) in German Gender Studies and Diversity Studies debates. The text analyses and highlights performative effects of a 'narrative of overcoming' according to which a multidimensional and non-hierarchic notion of diversity supersedes and replaces the critical concepts of gender and difference.

Introduction

Diversity, though deemed a concept that aims for social justice, has been called out for its lack of critical potential. Sara Ahmed has prominently

---

1   I wish to thank the two anonymous reviewers for engaging with this
     contribution and offering many truly helpful comments.

shown how declaring a commitment to diversity as an institutional speech act is a "non-performative" (Ahmed, 2012, p.116): it is a speech act that does not 'do as it says'. Thus, "the names come to stand in for the effects" (Ahmed, 2012, p.117). Similarly, Angela Davis states in her inaugural lecture at the Cornelia Goethe Center for Women's and Gender Studies in Frankfurt, Germany, in December 2013 that diversity in United States corporate as well as higher education contexts has come to stand for "a difference that makes no difference" (Davis, 2013). There seems to be a difference between what diversity is meant to mean, is meant to bring about, and what it actually brings about or has come to mean.

The skeptical evaluations of the (lack of) effects of diversity as a term for social justice that is fighting racialized discrimination and exclusion have traveled across geo-political contexts. While they certainly resonate with many other contexts, they are nevertheless also context-specific: Sara Ahmed's analysis outlines the critical potential of Whiteness Studies and antiracist commitment with regard to statements, academic literature, and actions in Australia, the United Kingdom, and the United States of America (Ahmed, 2004). Her further elaborations on 'saying diversity' as a non-performative speech act are based on research in the field of institutional diversity work in higher education in the UK and Australia (Ahmed, 2012). Angela Davis' statement in her lecture referred to equality politics in the USA. While these contexts have come to be of global relevance more so than many others, they nonetheless show specificity; the knowledges produced with regard to these contexts emerge together with the specific geo-political, social, institutional, and epistemological environments with which they engage; they come from somewhere, they "have a country" (Rich, 1985, p. 8).

This is not to say that they are irrelevant for other contexts. But when aiming for "politics of location" (Rich, 1985, p. 11) the specificities of the context of emergence and of travel need to be given some thought. For the German context it is necessary to reflect on the implications of a traveled concept or theory (Bal, 2002; Said, 1983) of diversity, which is often introduced as an English word into a German-speaking setting. Furthermore, the applicability of a traveled critique of this concept, e.g. as a non-performative and a difference that makes no difference needs to be considered. Additionally, both the affirmative reception of diversity terminology and its critical debating in Germany are seeping into other fields than that of equality politics and a more equal Human Resource Management. So, the travels of diversity also cross the boundaries of disciplines and fields of application.[2]The challenges faced by critics engaging with the concept of diversity in the German context are twofold: firstly, it is necessary to evaluate for the context of diversity politics and measures that intend to increase equality in which ways diversity may have brought the tendency not to 'say as it does' along with it and to point out where and when it is used as mere lip-service also in Germany. Secondly, it is necessary to focus on the specific effects that the introduction of the term diversity into a German setting brings about beyond not saying as it does, and to focus on the performativity of 'saying diversity' also beyond the context of equality politics. This contribution focuses on the latter task – which by no means implies that the former is not just as urgent.

Insisting that shifts in meaning brought about by the language of diversity do make differences, this paper examines in what way the practices of 'saying diversity' are involved in constituting a specific field of knowledge about diversity. The notion of performativity used here is leaning towards Judith Butler's and Michel Foucault's reading of discursive practice as proliferative. Butler's notion of performativity as "the reiterative and citational practice by which discourse produces the effect that it names" (Butler, 1993, p. 2) and Foucault's statement that discursive practices "systematically form the objects of which they speak" (Foucault, 1972, p. 49) share that discourse produces, discourse forms what can be said and thought, and it is contradictory

---

2   For an overview of the many meanings of a concept of diversity beyond the management of diversity in social sciences, cultural studies, and educational sciences, see e.g. Salzbrunn, 2014 and Walgenbach, 2014.

and proliferating. That is to say, the "effect that it names" and "the objects of which they speak" are not fixed but constantly on the move.[3]

My contribution focuses on the performative effects of academic storytelling practices (Haraway, 1989) with regard to diversity terminology in texts leaning towards diversity. I thus read narrative as one particular form of engagement in the formation of a discourse. In the stories told, statements about diversity's closeness or distance to concepts of gender on the one hand, and concepts of difference on the other will be highlighted. The latter two concepts seem to be chosen in order to negotiate the meaning of diversity, both in continuity with the field of Gender Studies, and also as markers of the differentiation of diversity from Gender Studies concepts.[4] These stories are seen as productive with regard to constituting and shaping a field of knowledge; they render certain knowledges acceptable and convincing and others problematic and limited.

After addressing the context of the discussion of diversity terminology in Germany, two central related story-lines will be highlighted below: first, a narrative of overcoming that has diversity emerging as the more 'up to date' term that replaces 'older' feminist terms and Gender Studies knowledge; second, an assertion of an all-encompassing non-hierarchic concept of diversity that supersedes a binary logic of difference. These

---

3   This specific version of performativity 'wants' something else than the notion of (non-)performativity enacted in Ahmed's engagement (Ahmed, 2004, p.50; Ahmed, 2012, pp.116ff.). Highlighting a contradictory discourse on diversity rather than evaluating the effects of the language of diversity in concrete equality politics necessitates another notion of performativity.

4   In "Against Proper Objects. Introduction" (Butler, 1994) Judith Butler shows how the new field of Lesbian and Gay Studies is similarly defined by way of focusing on certain concepts (sexuality, gender), which guarantee both continuity with Women's Studies, and difference from Women's Studies (Butler, 1994, p.2f.)

stories point at the problem of scholarly knowledge-making through overcoming and replacement, that is by way of casting away the old in order to install the new. Furthermore, they allow problematizing the specific knowledge that the examined diversity discourse constitutes.

Diversity Stories at Work

After the explicit appearance of the term diversity in Germany, a lot of output from the emerging field of Diversity Studies has been almost naïvely affirmative, more or less denying or downplaying all possible problematic effects of diversity terminology or diversity measurements while highlighting the potentials both for research and for increasing equal opportunity (especially Krell et al., 2007). Though claiming a strong tie between diversity and antidiscrimination work, the most visible contributions came from the field of Human Resource Management and they show a striking absence of references to earlier German feminist, queer, and antiracist activism and scholarly work, and particularly to contributions from People of Color and Black or Afro-German authors.[5] At the other end of the spectrum, the concept of diversity, or a "diversity dispositif" (Knapp, 2005), has been quickly rejected by Gender Studies and feminist scholars based on its supposed

---

5   The term People of Color is increasingly being used among activists and critical scholars in Germany as a political self-description for people who are subjected to racialization and exclusion by a dominant structure of *whiteness* in multiple different, at times contradictory ways (e.g. Ha, 2013). Identifications as Black German or Afro-German (Schwarze Deutsche or Afro-Deutsche, see e.g. Oguntoye, Opitz & Schultz, 1992) undermine the hegemonic racist imagination of German-ness as essentially *white* and as an identity that presumably cannot be acquired but has to be achieved by descent. 'Black' will be capitalized in order to highlight that it is meant to address a political self-identification rather than a biological categorization. For the role of Black women's and lesbian's activism for the Black movement in Germany, see e.g. Eggers 2010. For a collection of German contributions to Critical Whiteness Studies, see e.g. Eggers, Kilomba, Piesche & Arndt 2005.

profit-orientation, its reification of differences, and its neoliberal individualization of inequality (e.g. Knapp, 2005; Wetterer, 2002). Human Resource Management was not deemed a 'proper origin' for critical feminist thinking, and contributions from this field were received with suspicion (Putschert, 2007). The increasing popularity of diversity terminology was noted with worries about its future place in the academe that threatened to render Gender Studies and gender equality measurements obsolete, when this wide new umbrella term called diversity could, perhaps, house questions of gender alongside all other categorizations of difference. Against this competitive background, it seems that there was not much space left for a critical curiosity about the contradictory effects of diversity discourse in Germany.

Though the concept of diversity has increasingly been discussed (both in a problematizing as well as a partially affirmative manner) in connection with queer-feminist Gender Studies, intersectionality, postcoloniality and decolonization (e.g. Smykalla & Vinz, 2011; Dhawan & Castro Varela, 2011; Engel, 2013), the tensions in the relation between gender and diversity are still far from resolved. The debates are characterized by contradiction and conflicts among activists and scholars; conflicts about who gets to define the scope of Gender Studies, who gets to represent a field, who is structurally excluded by institutional *whiteness*[6] in teaching and hiring practices, whose visibility is erased in publications etc.

In the context of German academic research, both the concept of intersectionality and of diversity threaten to become a buzzing thing that *white* scholars can discuss to reform their teaching and researching agenda, without these engagements necessarily showing any effects in terms of changing the distribution of power in the academe (Gutiérrez-Rodríguéz, 2011). It has been noted with regard to intersectionality that German scholars may erase Black feminist work

---

6   I put *whiteness* in italics to mark the term as referring to a structural distribution of power.

in their contributions; they manage to write about intersectionality without ever mentioning the work of Black feminist scholars, or suggest versions of intersectionality without mentioning racism or structural *whiteness* (Bilge, 2013; Chebout, 2011). The dominance of *white* German voices from the field of Human Resource Management in what claims to be Diversity Studies mirrors this phenomenon. The texts I am critically discussing in this paper in turn mirror and repeat this claim for dominance – an unfortunate effect of exposing the ways in which they work.

In the face of the complicated context that I can only hint at here, it is necessary to consider that it is not so clear what is actually being said and what may be promised in the German context, when 'diversity' is being said. Whereas in the US and UK contexts, it seems that 'diversity' cannot really be said without thinking 'antiracism,' in Germany it happens quite frequently that examples for successful diversity work are given that do not address racialized discrimination and exclusion at all. In Germany, then, it is quite possible to 'say diversity,' without ever mentioning 'race'. Thus 'saying diversity' can even erase the struggles against racialized discrimination and systematic exclusion of racialized 'others,' rather than strengthen them (see also Thompson & Zablotzky in this volume). Analyzing what it is that is said or done when 'saying diversity' is a necessary component of any evaluation of diversity's effects.

In this vein, the following two sections show in what way stories told in academic texts are involved in rendering a specific reading of diversity plausible and self-evident. The given readings de-familiarize the acceptability of the offered positions and allow thinking about diversity stories as performative, as constituting diversity as a specific field of knowledge, and as claiming disciplinary and conceptual space in a particular way. Thinking about these claims *as claims* will allow for the contestation of their legitimacy.

The readings below are based on detailed text analyses undertaken during my PhD-research on the emerging discourse on diversity in Germany (Marten, 2014; Marten, forthcoming). Against the backdrop of a Foucaultian notion of critique and genealogy (Foucault, 1997, 1984), text examples are analyzed with regard to the role of narrative (Bal, 2009; White, 1981) in negotiating the critical potential of diversity terminology and the relationship between diversity and gender, and diversity and difference. The persuasiveness of the matter-of-fact stories is thus put into question and their effects can be better problematized. The text examples (Krell, 2009; Krell et al., 2007; Sieben & Bornheim, 2011; Smykalla & Vinz, 2011; Vinz & Schiederig, 2010) affirmatively express support for diversity terminology and for Diversity Studies as a promising new disciplinary space.[7] The relationship between diversity, gender, and difference is negotiated by way of identifying (either shared or divergent) historical *origins*[8] and trajectories for the respective concepts.[9]

---

7   In this paper, I am focusing on only 'one side of the story'. The particular depiction of the relation between diversity and gender given in the here discussed examples was strongly rejected, especially from the perspective of feminist theory, see e.g. Knapp, 2005; Purtschert, 2007; Wetterer, 2002. In my dissertation, the ways in which diversity is critically debated are foregrounded (Marten 2014; Marten, forthcoming). In this contribution, the things that are possibly 'done' when 'saying diversity' affirmatively were of higher concern.

8   The word *origin* is put in italics to highlight that it is the very notion of an origin, of un-equivocally identifiable origins for present concepts or phenomena, and the assumption of their subsequent continuous progressive movement through time, that is put into question in a Foucaultian perspective of genealogy that follows Nietzsche's notions of descent and emergence (Foucault, 1984, pp.80ff.).

9   The texts are utilized as cases with which I can illustrate a problem to think with. As cases, they relate to the discursive fields in which they are written and read, but they do not represent a field, nor is it my intention to prove to what degree they may stand for a dominant perspective, nor have I collected quantitative data on whether they represent a character of debate that is specific to the time-span of publication.

Diversity as the Modernizer of Gender

The text examples propagate the institutionalization of Diversity Studies, and/or a concept of diversity as a central category for analysis. Distance and proximity between gender and diversity[10] are negotiated by way of a contradictory play between continuity and discontinuity. Nevertheless, recurring story-lines can be highlighted. I use 'story-line' where Mieke Bal uses "fabula" as "a series of logically and chronologically related events that are caused and experienced by actors." (Bal, 2009, p. 5) The analysis below does not aim to speculate about possible intentions of authors, but focuses on processes of stabilization and producing acceptability of fact-like knowledge by way of narrative passages, which work towards the plausibilization of (located, particular) perspectives as common sense (White, 1981, pp. 3).

In the text examples diversity and gender are portrayed on the level of description as belonging to a shared conceptual space and as sharing similar interests. A "functional marriage" (Krell, 2009, p. 33) is suggested between diversity and gender, because both approaches are seen to share interests and concepts, while they only differ with regard to the concrete measures. Metaphors of a mutual opening of doors or of offering tailwind for one another are used to describe the character of the relationship between diversity and gender (Krell et al., 2007, p.12; Krell, 2009, p. 141; Vinz & Schiederig, 2010, p. 32). According to Bal, metaphors and substantives can be read as mini-narratives (Bal, 2009, pp. 35, pp. 158). The mentioned metaphors tell stories

---

10 The exact meanings of the terms diversity and gender remain blurry in the text examples: they can refer to concepts and categories of knowledge, to analytical categories for sociological research, and to strategies and measurements for the increase of equal opportunity or the reduction of discrimination and inequality. I will not resolve this lack of precision, because it does not, or at least not only, lead to a miscommunication, but seems rather productive with regard to the emergence of a convincing story about, and a discursive field around the concept of diversity.

about potentially helping one another into a space that is otherwise locked, about helping each other across a threshold, assuming a realm of shared precariousness and marginality on the same side of the threshold.

A common historically grown commitment to antidiscrimination is mentioned as the ground for similar interests (Sieben & Bornheim, 2011, p. 96; Vinz & Schiederig, 2010, p. 26). Diversity is here often introduced as a direct offspring of the US civil rights movement and as the continuation of affirmative action measures (Sieben & Bornheim, 2011, p. 96; Vinz & Schiederig, 2010, p. 26). Critical viewpoints about the introduction of diversity terminology in the US context (e.g. Edelman et al., 2001) are being omitted in these statements about the supposed *origin* of diversity in the struggles against discrimination. Contradictions are thus erased in the narrative assertion of a shared interest between gender and diversity.

Finally, diversity is brought into conceptual contact with the proliferation and multiplication of the scope of gender in queer-feminist Women's and Gender Studies, and also with the reflections on interlocking systems of oppression and a multiplication of axes of difference that are considered relevant in intersectional approaches (Krell et al., 2007, pp. 8, pp. 12; Vinz & Schiederig, 2010, p. 20). This closeness is generally merely asserted and claimed as the background for another argument, rather than elaborated on, or argued for itself. It thus emerges as an accepted fact, not as a contestable reading.

These declarations of commonality between diversity and gender will now be contrasted with a narrative about the overcoming and replacement of the *old* (gender) by the *new* (diversity). In an introductory text on gender and diversity Vinz and Schiederig (2010) give a short historical narration. This narration deals with the "struggle for women's rights" (p. 19) at the beginning of a subchapter on gender in the style of giving relevant background knowledge and facts. This style of giving the 'background facts' is achieved by way of giving information without discernible perspective of a narrator, by referring to 'history' as a frame of reference, and by leaving out explanations on the methods with which the given knowledge was produced (Bal, 2009, pp.26, White, 1981, pp. 3; see also Haraway's "god trick" (Haraway, 1988, p. 582). The following account of the struggle for women's rights is given:

> Already in the 18th century the first women's movement formed, which demanded the introduction of the right to vote also for women. [...] In the late 1960s the second women's movement began. The third women's movement formed in the 1990s. (Vinz & Schiederig, 2010, pp.19; my translation)

This embedded historical retroversion into the past of gender can be read as the background against which the primary story about gender and diversity takes place in the text (Bal, 2009, pp. 58, p. 82). The women's movement and the question of gender are presented as historical matters, as things that have passed, that are of the past. The movements of the past and their concepts seem to only prepare the subsequent passages on diversity in the text. The style of historically correct reporting allows little doubt about that which is reported on. A contradictory field is here being portrayed as an orderly series of clearly identifiable waves or phases that the women's movements stand for. Even though this particular way of narrating identity and continuity is very common, presenting the series of phases of the German women's movements as a linear progression nonetheless covers over and obscures the multiplicity of the debates that took place in any one of these phases.

The passage about the women's movements is positioned in an introductory subchapter on the concept of gender before the primary story arrives at the central subchapters on the concept of diversity. The section on diversity begins with the sentence: "The concept of diversity encompasses additional dimensions of difference besides gender" (Vinz & Schiederig, 2010, p. 26; my translation). Diversity is here posited as conceptually broader than gender, as encompassing more differences.

Diversity then seems to be *more* than gender can be. This notion of gender as "only gender" and diversity as multidimensional is prepared in the fragment about the women's movements and given the appearance of facticity. This is accomplished by way of a narrative strategy, which Clare Hemmings called "glossing" (Hemmings, 2011, p. 39). The brief passage on the women's movements reduces the multiplicity and the contradictions in the (many, not always harmoniously united) women's movements by way of condensing long periods of time into tell-able phases of one-and-the-same movement. These phases in turn are assigned an identity – in this case, unsurprisingly, there are three phases of women's movements, which are assigned one central problem or concept each. The text proceeds:

> With the three waves of the women's movement three different theoretical approaches are connected. Whereas the first wave focused on equal rights for women, the second wave supported a "difference feminism," which assumed differences between women and men and demanded the advancement of women. [...] The feminist Women's Studies were criticized for generalizing the experience of white middle class women and for neglecting the differences among the group of women (class, ethnicity, age). The third wave tries to do justice to this critique and by and large supports a deconstructive approach, which regards gender as a social construction and accordingly demands a consideration of gender-specific problems in all measures. (Vinz & Schiederig, 2010, p. 20; my translation)

Three waves are described following three different angles: equality, difference, deconstruction (Vinz & Schiederig, 2010, pp. 19). It is noteworthy that in the third wave the demands for recognition of differences among women (here: class, ethnicity, age) that should be considered in feminist Women's Studies merges with deconstruction. Conflicts between the mentioned demands for recognition and the practice of deconstruction are made invisible. The critics who demand the consideration of other grammars of difference remain implicit in the passive voice; they do not appear as subjects, and their criticism is merely the motor for a reformed third wave of feminism; their criticism is narratively eaten up by an ever-evolving chain of women's movements. Clare Hemmings describes similarly how Black feminist work has been integrated and reduced to merely a catalyzing phase that improves Western post-structuralist feminism in Western feminist texts (Hemmings, 2011, pp. 40). The quoted passage additionally does not differentiate between deconstruction and social construction. Despite ample lack of clarity, the absence of the narrative perspective from which these statements are made has them appear as historical facts that seemingly speak for themselves (White, 1981, p. 3).

The narration of a chronological sequence of identifiable phases of the development of the women's movement is connected with a logic of causality: The phases of the women's movement are explained as resulting from their historical circumstances, their contexts, which led to a specific focus in the respective waves. The historical contexts, that is to say 'the facts,' seem to demand these particular developments of movements and their concepts. It is the critique of the second wave that is the motor of change, which led to the specific formation of the third wave. The replacement of an older phase by a new phase is thus portrayed as necessary and coherent.

The embedded story about history connects with the primary argument of the text. The description of the third wave of the women's movement draws on the criticism of white and middle class positions and the resulting multiplication of grammars of difference in the concept of gender, as was and is discussed in connection with the notion of intersectionality or interdependency elsewhere (e.g. Walgenbach, 2012). In the text example this potential complexity is depicted as resulting in

> a deconstructive approach, which regards gender
> as a social construction and accordingly demands a

consideration of gender-specific problems in all measures.
(Vinz & Schiederig, 2010, p. 20; my translation)

The concept of gender appears as "a social construction" by way of the "glossing" of the third phase that simplifies the above-mentioned ongoing complicated debates within Gender Studies about the interdependent character of categorizations of difference. This narrow concept of gender, then, in fact encompasses less than the concept of diversity, which is characterized as multidimensional in the text. The evaluation of the concepts' usefulness with regard to a characterization of the current society as multiple and diverse anticipates the overcoming of (this particular notion of) gender already in the catchy opening phrase of the text-example: "Diversity is growing in our society" (Vinz & Schiederig, 2010, p. 13). Diversity is suggested as the tool with which the complexity of current increasingly heterogeneous societies can be better analyzed, while gender seems to only capture one of the many relevant differences. In sum, parallel to the asserted common grounds between gender and diversity the text tells a story about the necessary overcoming and replacement of a dated concept of gender by the more up to date concept of diversity. This narrative of overcoming rests on a linear-chronological and causal image of time and progress. This notion of time and/as progress in turn operates through reductive identification of unequivocal generations of concepts.

The Narrative Disappearance of Hierarchies

The distinctions between diversity and gender in the diversity texts at hand connect with a narration on diversity and difference. In the texts in question, the term diversity is used in connection with positive connotations, with enriching variation and multiplicity, described with words that sound 'nice'. Krell et al. (2007) explain the meaning of diversity with these synonyms:

Diversity – respectively in German plurality, diversity, the manifold or similar [...]. (Krell et al., 2007, p. 8; my translation)

Vinz and Schiederig similarly define diversity as more than a mere description of phenomena of difference. Diversity, to them, is a concept with a positive, affirmative character that adds appreciation to description:

the concept of diversity, exceeding the mere description of heterogeneity and difference, carries a positive connotation of enrichment, of more options and choices, of lively diversity as opposed to the monotony of homogeneity. (Vinz & Schiederig, 2010, p. 26; my translation)

The concept of diversity captures differences and similarities (Krell & Sieben, 2010, p.50), that is to say that assessing diversity is not only about the harsh opposites, about that which separates irreconcilably, but also about that which connects people across/through their differences. In accordance with such a dynamic notion of difference, authors describe identities as shifting and multiple (Krell & Sieben, 2010, p. 50; Krell et al., 2007, p. 10).

This notion of a multiplicity of diverse locations is posited in a conceptual conflict or tension with the concept of difference, which here boils down to the hierarchic character of difference. Diversity, in similarity to a "democratic concept of difference" (Krell, 2009, p. 140), is said to be striving to overcome hierarchic difference. Smykalla and Vinz similarly refer to the notion of diversity as striving for a horizontal approach in antidiscrimination politics assuming a "non-hierarchic-diversity" (Smykalla & Vinz, 2011, p. 11). Vinz and Schiederig stress that it is possible and desirable for diversity concepts to

think diversity in such a manner, so that it questions
the binary logic of differentiation and opens itself for a
multiple understanding of identity (Vinz & Schiederig,
2010, p. 31; my translation).

The text examples not only question or problematize a binary logic of
differentiation, though. Rather, they tell a story about diversity and
difference that identifies the concept of difference with the troublesome
hierarchic binary logic of differentiation. Whereas diversity is connected
with plurality and an affirmative character of appreciation, difference is
generally introduced as synonymous with alterity, with a distance from
a normative identity, or with constructions of 'otherness'. Krell et al.
accordingly group the concept of difference together with terms that
all describe 'otherness':

> Aside of difference, the terms alterity, otherness,
> foreignness/strangeness (Fremdheit) [...] and similar also
> are to be mentioned here. (Krell et al., 2007, p. 8; my
> translation)

Similarly, Vinz and Schiederig introduce the concept of difference
as referring to the process of 'othering' and to binary hierarchic
classifications embedded in relations of power (Vinz & Schiederig,
2010, pp. 29). By way of framing diversity as positive and as valuing
differences, and by equating the concept of difference with the negative
result of relations of power and 'othering,' the following statement can
be made in their text:

> How can diversity be thought, without increasing
> difference? (Vinz & Schiederig, 2010, p. 30; my
> translation)

This statement carries a message on two levels: on the level of difference
and diversity as concepts and approaches to analyze, describe and criticize
society as structured through differentiation on the one hand, and on

the level of difference and diversity as stand-ins for the actual 'social reality' on the other. While diversity becomes a stand-in for appreciated, celebrated differences, difference is portrayed as a concept that not only focuses on analyzing the problems caused by hierarchic processes of 'othering,' but simultaneously stands for the 'real' social differences that are hierarchically ordered. The problematic hierarchic character of differences should, according to the quote, not be increased, and should not be called into being, when thinking 'diversity'. The juxtaposition of appreciated diversity with problematic difference connotes the notion of difference with an 'otherness' that causes problems, that crosses the lines of tolerance, and that, perhaps, according to the quoted passage should also not be increased? Reversely, the normative and affirmative approach that the concept of diversity follows comes to 'be' a diverse world of happy multiplicity: what diversity wants to achieve already seems to be assumed as a given by way of using the right concept to look at the world. This dynamic in diversity discourse clearly connects with Ahmed's diagnosis of diversity as a non-performative with regard to diversity politics in higher education. But here it is taken from the context of managing diversity to the level of imagining and analyzing social relations.

The positing of diversity as non-hierarchic-diversity in opposition to difference as only addressing and reifying hierarchic axes of exclusion resonates with the developmental narrative I have described above with regard to gender: diversity is articulated as the more advanced concept for the current tasks in a multiple and flexible globalized world, where in/exclusions seem to happen in a much more complicated way than the old imagination of the binary would allow to grasp. This version of the story about diversity overcoming an older concept, a binary concept of difference, is, again, based on a reductive conceptual identification of difference with one particular very limiting notion of difference. And the identification of difference as only a 'binary-hierarchic difference' is in turn connected with a temporal phase, which is (necessarily) over: the days of the binary as an explanatory model are numbered.

The proposed appreciation of diversity as the horizontal embrace of all sorts of differences seems infinite and differences seem valuable for no specific reason; they are valuable because they 'are'. Despite the suggested infinity of diversity's inclusiveness, the analyzed texts themselves introduce limits to how far the appreciation and embrace of diversity can go:

> Here [regarding the productive processing of diversity; E.M.] it is always also relevant to ask which degree of difference is *still legitimate* for society, and where and by whom the boundaries are being drawn. (Vinz & Schiederig, 2010, p. 26; my emphasis)

"Unterschiedlichkeit" is being used in this passage, rather than "Vielfalt", therefore I have translated it as "difference" – a move which of course is productive with regard to making my point more plausible. This quote then suggests that diversity, when it becomes difference, can exceed the legitimate range of acceptability in a society. It can seemingly be 'enough' and it can be 'too much to take'. The question in the passage does not seem to be so much about whether boundaries of legitimacy are to be set, but where they are to be set. Thus it is rendered legitimate that there is illegitimate difference, if by degree or kind, that exceeds that which a society can be asked to tolerate.

Instead of buying into the happy tale according to which an appreciative version of diversity has indeed overcome the marking and exclusion of unwanted differences, it seems more plausible that appreciated diversity rests on an implicit (constitutive?) outside: intolerable unwanted differences, non-valued differences, differences that are construed as harmful or unproductive. Davina Cooper (2004) has shown for the context of the UK that the valued forms of diversity emerge against the background of de-valued differences connoted with social harm. Thomas Hylland Eriksen (2006) has argued for the Norwegian context that appreciated diversity is necessarily accompanied by its 'other': the unwanted differences of those who seem to refuse Western, neoliberal values of tolerance, fragmentation and flexibility. Sara Ahmed (2012) writes about the celebration of 'digestible' diversity that brings about the specter of an indigestible difference as its 'other'. A similar skepticism has been discussed in Germany predominantly with regard to Diversity Management. Diversity Management measures have been criticized for necessarily selecting productive, valuable difference in order to meet their ultima ratio: profitability (Meuser, 2013; Purtschert, 2007). Thus, they cannot prioritize social justice (which may not come as such a great surprise), but only integrate and value certain 'others,' as long as their integration increases the creativity and optimizes the performance of businesses (ibid.).

This suspicion towards an overall inclusive impetus of the language of diversity must be extended and addressed also to a concept of diversity as is suggested for critical research and for diversity strategies beyond the business-case of Diversity Management. The notion of affirmative and appreciative diversity *itself* always already carries the question of value: which differences are welcomed, appreciated and valued in what contexts, to what degree with what effects? What is deemed tolerable, what is 'across the lines,' and who is it that gets to draw the lines? In order to ask these questions it is helpful not to do away with the concept of difference altogether, but to be able to return to the different conceptual levels that can be addressed with it, among which are the questions of (binary and not so binary) hierarchies.

Conclusion

The given analyses show how the stories told in German academic texts affirming (a certain kind of) diversity terminology convince by way of telling a narrative of overcoming that installs diversity as the modernizer of (a certain notion of) gender and difference. De-familiarizing the common sense mobilized in the plausible stories told in the text examples allows questioning the 'facts' presented as 'facts,' and as the foundation of the arguments given.

With regard to the German context, many questions about the effects of diversity discourse have not yet been asked, much less answered. The analysis offered in this paper suggests that 'saying diversity' beyond the context of diversity politics and equality measurements produces effects, yet not necessarily in the ways it was perhaps intended to. The stories told about diversity are productive and performative in the sense of constituting a field of knowledge about diversity in a particular way. Looking at them as claims and as discursive interventions that speak from somewhere, that "have a country" (Rich, 1985, p. 8), allows contesting their generalizing scope.

The necessary wariness of diversity as a possible, or perhaps even likely, non-performative with regard to institutional equality politics should not invite German critical scholars to overlook the complicated setting in which diversity 'lands,' and the contradictory effects that it produces: imaginations of diversity as well as concepts for a critical analysis of social phenomena matter; they bring about effects, and they make differences. Looking at the performative effects of diversity as proliferative of course also implies that it is on the move, that its meaning can be contested and struggled over, and that other stories can be told. What diversity can 'be' or 'do' in the future cannot yet be said, but, perhaps, it can be co-created in a critical debate characterized by curiosity for contradiction, and in the telling of many different stories.

References

Ahmed, S. (2004). Declarations of whiteness. The non-performativity of anti-racism. *Borderlands*, 3(2). http://www.borderlands.net.au/ vol3no2_2004/ahmed_declarations.htm (last accessed 12/18/2015).

Ahmed, S. (2012). *On being included. Racism and diversity in institutional life*. Durham/London: Duke University Press.

Bal, M. (2002). *Travelling concepts in the humanities. A rough guide*. Toronto/Buffalo/London: University of Toronto Press.

Bal, M. (2009). *Narratology. Introduction to the theory of Narrative* (3rd ed.). Toronto/Buffalo/London: University of Toronto Press.

Bilge, S. (2013). Intersectionality undone. Saving intersectionality from feminist intersectionality studies. *DuBois Review*, 10(2), 405-423.

Butler, J. (1993). *Bodies that matter. On the discursive limits of "sex"*. New York/London: Routledge.

Butler, J. (1994). Against proper objects. Introduction. *differences: A Journal of Feminist Cultural Studies*, 6(2+3), 1-26.

Chebout, L. N. (2011). Wo ist Intersectionality in bundesdeutschen Intersektionalitätsdiskursen? Exzerpte aus dem Reisetagebuch einer Traveling Theory. In Smykalla, S. & Vinz, D. (Eds.), *Intersektionalität zwischen Gender und Diversity. Theorien, Methoden und Politiken der Chancengleichheit* (pp. 46-60). Münster: Westfälisches Dampfboot.

Cooper, D. (2004). *Challenging diversity: Rethinking equality and the value of difference.* Cambridge: Cambridge University Press.

Davis, A. (2013). Inaugural Speech for the Angela Davis guest professorship at Cornelia Goethe Centre at Frankfurt University. http://www.cgc.uni-Frankfurt.de/feminismabolition.shtml (last accessed 12/13/15).

Dhawan, N. & Castro Varela, M. (Eds.) (2011). *Soziale (Un) Gerechtigkeit. Kritische Perspektiven auf Diversity, Intersektionalität und Antidiskriminierung.* Münster/Berlin: LIT Verlag.

Edelman, L. B., Fuller, S. R. & Mara-Drita, I. (2001). Diversity rhetoric and the managerialization of law. In *American Journal of Sociology,* 106(6), 1589-1641.

Eggers, M. M., Kilomba, G., Piesche, P. & Arndt S. (Eds.). (2005). *Mythen, Masken und Subjekte. Kritische Weißseinsforschung in Deutschland.* Münster: Unrast.

Eggers, M.M. (2010). Knowledges of (un)belonging: Epistemic change as a defining mode for black women's activism in Germany. In U. Lindner, M. Möhring, M. Stein & S. Stroh (Eds.), *Hybrid cultures - Nervous states: Britain and Germany in a (post)colonial world* (pp. 189-202). Amsterdam & New York: Rodopi.

Engel, A. (2013). Lust auf Komplexität. Gleichstellung, Antidiskriminierung und die Strategie des Queerversity. *Feministische Studien,* 1, 39-45.

Eriksen, T. H. (2006). Diversity versus difference: Neoliberalism in the minority-debate. In Rottenburg, R., Schnepel, B. & Shimana, S. (Eds.), *The making and unmaking of differences. Anthropological, sociological and philosophical perspectives* (pp. 13-25). Bielefeld: Transcript.

Foucault, M. (1972). *The archeology of knowledge*. London: Tavistock.

Foucault, M. (1997). What is critique? In Lotringer, S. (Ed.), *The politics of truth* (pp. 41-82). L.A.: Semiotext(e).

Foucault, M. (1984). Nietzsche, history, genealogy. In Rabinow, P. (Ed.), *The Foucault reader* (pp. 76–100). New York: Pantheon Books.

Gutiérrez-Rodríguéz, E. (2011). Intersektionalität oder: Wie nicht über Rassismus sprechen? In Hess, S., Langreiter, N. & Timm, E. (Eds.), *Intersektionalität revisited: Empirische, theoretische und methodische Erkundungen* (pp. 77-99). Bielefeld: Transcript.

Ha, K. N. (2013). ‚People of color' als Diversity-Ansatz in der antirassistischen Selbstbenennungs- und Identitäts-politik. https://heimatkunde.boell.de/2009/11/01/people-color-als-diversity-ansatz-der-antirassistischen-selbstbenennungs-und

Haraway, D. J. (1988). Situated knowledges: The science question in feminism and the privilege of partial perspective. *Feminist Studies*, 14(3), 575-599.

Haraway, D. J. (1989). *Primate visions. Gender, race, and nature in the world of modern science*. New York & London: Routledge.

Hemmings, C. (2011). *Why stories matter. The political grammar of feminist theory*. Durham/London: Duke University Press.

Knapp, G. (2005). Intersectionality - ein neues Paradigma feministischer Theorie? Zur transatlantischen Reise von Race, Class, Gender. *Feministische Studien*, 1, 68-81.

Krell, G. (2009). Gender und Diversity: Eine ‚Vernunftehe' – Plädoyer für vielfältige Verbindungen. In Andresen, S., Koreuber, M- & Lüdke, D. (Eds.), *Gender und Diversity: Albtraum oder Traumpaar? Interdisziplinärer Dialog zur "Modernisierung" von Geschlechter- und Gleichstellungs-politik* (pp. 133-154). Wiesbaden: VS Verlag.

Krell, G., Riedmüller, B., Sieben, B. & Vinz, D. (2007). Einleitung: Diversity Studies als integrierende Forschungsrichtung. In Krell et al. (Eds.), *Diversity Studies. Grundlagen und disziplinäre Ansätze* (pp. 7-16), Frankfurt/New York: Campus.

Marten, E. (2014). *Diversity stories: Contested genealogies: Re-writing diversity's present at the crossroads of German gender studies and diversity studies*, unpublished dissertation, Universität Hamburg.

Marten, E (forthcoming). *Genealogies and conceptual belonging. Zones of interference between gender and diversity*. Research in Gender and Society Series. Research Monograph. London/New York: Routledge.

Meuser, M. (2013). Diversity Management – Anerkennung von Vielfalt? In Pries, L. (Ed.), *Zusammenhalt durch Vielfalt? Bindungskräfte der Vergesellschaftung im 21. Jahrhundert* (pp. 167-176). Wiesbaden: Springer VS.

Oguntoye, K., Opitz, M. & Schultz, D. (Eds.) (1992). *Farbe Bekennen. Afro-deutsche Frauen auf den Spuren ihrer Geschichte*. Frankfurt a.M.: Fischer.

Purtschert, P. (2007). Diversity Management: Mehr Gewinn durch weniger Diskriminierung? Von der Differenz im Umgang mit Differenzen. *Femina Politica*, 16(1), 88-96.

Rich, A. (1985). Notes toward a politics of location. In Diaz-Diocaretz, M. & Zavala, I. M. (Eds.), *Women, feminist identity, and society in the 1980s: Selected papers* (pp. 7-22). Amsterdam/Philadelphia: John Benjamins Publishing Company.

Said, E. (1983/2014). *The world, the text, and the critic*. Cambridge: Harvard UP. Salzbrunn, M. *Vielfalt/Diversität*. Bielefeld: Transcript.

Sieben, B. & Bornheim, N. (2011). Intersektionalität und Diversity – Achsen der Differenz in Management-konzepten und Managementforschung. In Smykalla, S. & Vinz, D. (Eds.), *Intersektionalität zwischen Gender und Diversity. Theorien, Methoden und Politiken der Chancengleichheit* (pp. 93-110). Münster: Westfälisches Dampfboot.

Smykalla, S. & Vinz, D. (2011). Einleitung. Geschlechter-forschung und Gleichstellungspolitiken vor neuen theoretischen, methodologischen und politischen Herausforderungen. In Ibid. (Eds.), *Intersektionalität zwischen Gender und Diversity. Theorien, Methoden und Politiken der Chancengleichheit* (pp. 9-19). Münster: Westfälisches Dampfboot.

Thompson, V. E. & Zablotsky, V. (2016). Rethinking Diversity in Academic Institutions – For a Repoliticization of Difference as a Matter of Social Justice. *Wagadu. A Journal of Transnational Women's and Gender Studies*, 16, 76-94.

Vinz, D. & Schiederig, K. (2010). Gender und Diversity: Vielfalt verstehen und gestalten. In Massing, P. (Ed.), *Gender und Diversity. Vielfalt verstehen und gestalten* (pp. 13-44). Schwalbach/Ts.: Wochenschau-Verlag.

Walgenbach, K. (2012). Intersektionalität – Eine Einführung. http://portal-intersektionalitaet.de/theoriebildung/schluesseltexte/walgenbach-einfuehrung/

Walgenbach, Katharina (2014). *Heterogenität – Intersektionalität – Diversity in der Erziehungswissenschaft*. Opladen/Toronto: Barbara Budrich.

Wetterer, A. (2002). Strategien rhetorischer Modernisierung. Gender Mainstreaming, Managing Diversity und die Professionalisierung der Gender Expertinnen. In *Zeitschrift für Frauenforschung und Geschlechterstudien*, 20(3), 129-148.

White, H. (1981). The value of narrativity in the representation of reality. In Mitchell, W.J.T. (Ed.), *On narrative* (pp. 1-23). Chicago & London: University of Chicago Press.

SEVEN

(NON-) SPEECH ACTS: THE PERFORMATIVE POWER OF SILENCE

Jane Chin Davidson
California State University, San Bernadino

Correspondence: Jane Chin Davidson, California State University, San Bernadino
Janechindavidson@alumni.reed.edu

Abstract

Judgment of accented speech as "inferior English" or "immigrant speech" reinforces an aural type of racial discrimination, especially in the political context of education and the state. The institutional silencing of "defective" speech substantiates the practice of self-silencing in which the (non-) speech act functions as a phenomenological engagement and as a non-performativity of racial difference.

Intersectional critique emerged in the aftermath of Anita Hill's spoken testimony exposing the sexual harassment she experienced as a law clerk for Justice Clarence Thomas during his 1991 Supreme Court confirmation hearings. Hill's personal telling and the subsequent "hearing" by the legislators was a major disruption to the status quo of American politics since the high stakes for race and gender were played out on the civic stage for electing the Justice to the U.S. Supreme Court.

As a witness in the public forum, Hill's *speech act* ultimately revealed the ways in which women of color were subordinated by both feminist and critical-race initiatives[1](Crenshaw, 1991). And yet, no amount of political debate holds as much promise for the cause of civil rights as confirming a judge who embodies the raced subject himself, who potentially speaks on behalf of the non-white constituency. Twenty-five years later, however, Justice Thomas's speech act in *not* speaking during his term on the bench has garnered the most attention, posing the question as to why he has been largely silent (Cohen, 2013; Liptak, 2013; McGough, 2014). In order for legal debate to occur, deliberations of the Supreme Court must be conducted through the spoken word; and thus, Thomas's withholding from oral arguments since 2006 is considered a remarkable period of silence. He made news in 2013 when he finally spoke out in court, although his brief remark was inaudible overall: his utterance, "well – he did not," was the fragment recorded in the court transcript (Liptak, 2013; McGough, 2014). Thomas's influence on the legislative process is now historicized by the event of his *non-speech act*, his *not* giving voice to his constituents as the second African-American Justice to be confirmed in the history of the Court. Jacques Derrida (1992, p.13) explains that the role of speech constitutes the "very emergence of justice and law, the founding and justifying moment that institutes law implies a performative force, which is always an interpretative force."

In addressing "Difference that makes no Difference" for this special issue of *Wagadu*, the "(non-)speech act" provides another context for reviewing the non-performativity of intersectionality and diversity, particularly within the political economy of state institutions, civic forums and education. The important outcome of Hill's testimony was the development of intersectionality and Kimberlé Crenshaw's exposure of the absence of advocacy for women of color (Adewunmi, 2014). The (non-)impact of Hill's speech act on both legislative and judicial institutions was highly influential in the 1990s feminist discourse, and twenty-five years later, a return to this longstanding civic context for analyzing speech and power shifts the focus toward Thomas's inexplicable silence on the Supreme Court bench. The (non-)speech act constitutes the negative properties of the speech act, the opposite of J.L. Austin's emphasis on the contractual "I do, I swear" of performative utterances that are ritually and socially conventional and yet function as legally binding acts within the civic institution (Austin, 1962). Based on the expansion of the meaning of the speech act, defined by utterances, illocutionary force, and the "need to be heard," the aim of this study is to investigate institutional silencing in relation to self-silencing as exemplified by Thomas.

In the broader scope of *silencing acts*, the detrimental effects can be examined by looking at judgments of racial and sexual biases found in educational processes that are ultimately legislated state processes. A clear public case for examining institutional silencing emerges with the recent elimination of the voice given to Mexican Americans under Arizona's 2010 House Bill 2281. The bill not only prohibits public schools from teaching material focused on a particular ethnic group, but also removes Spanish-speaking teachers with "heavy accents" from their teaching positions in Arizona schools (Jordan, 2010). The legislation of accented speech has brought exposure and attention to a particular instrumentalization of the silencing act. Linguists have conducted studies in the aftermath of Arizona's ruling revealing the racially determined biases and judgments toward "immigrant accents" attributed to primarily Mexican and Asian-American speakers. Accented speech involves a greater range of impacts and associations for defining the (non-)speech act. When viewed in the greater institutional context, the silencing of accented speech is at once a phenomenological *and* a juridical act.

Inspired by Sara Ahmed's definition of "diversity work as a practical phenomenology" (Ahmed, 2012, p.173), this study on the (non-)speech act contributes to research on performance theory and feminist materialism as a development of linguistics and philosophy. Ahmed's reading of phenomenology engages Husserl's reorientation of the "worldly" as a conception of philosophy that moves away from simply a "reflection on the world" towards a theory that actually transforms existence. She adds to this philosophical equation "the Marxist understanding" in which "the point of intellectual labor" is to change the world and not simply to interpret the world (ibid., p.174). The new approach to feminist materialism recognizes the ways in which performances of language – in relation to race, gender, and sexuality – affect material consequences. For instance, Ahmed visualizes the frustrating efforts that diversity workers endure by describing the "physical and emotional labor of 'banging your head against a brick wall'" in her reconceptualization of the metaphorical "wall" that constitutes a material "barrier that is solid and tangible in the present, a barrier to change as well as to the mobility of some, a barrier that remains invisible to those who can flow into the spaces created by institutions." (Ahmed, 2012, p.175) Likewise, the rhetorical use of the "wall" by Donald Trump in his 2016 campaign promise to "build a great, great wall" along the Mexico-U.S. border illustrates Ahmed's materialist barrier as one that circumscribes the Mexican immigrant through the stereotype of "drugs, crime, and rapists" (what Trump asserts his wall will keep out) (Gabbatt, 2015). According to Diana Coole and Samantha Frost, the paradoxical distinction of "immaterial things" such as "language, consciousness, subjectivity, agency, mind, soul," expands the new materialist category that also includes "imagination, emotions, values, [and] meaning" (2010, p.2). Today's feminist materialism has moved on from the 1990s debates instigated by Marxist critics such as Martha Nussbaum and Nancy Fraser (Fraser, 1990; Nussbaum, 1999) who contested the poststructuralist approaches often attributed to Judith Butler's feminist performance theory (Butler, 1988). As Nussbaum asserts, Butler's theorizing of speech acts, psychic life and gender performance tells women that "they need not work on changing the law, or feeding the hungry, or assailing power through theory harnessed to material politics" (1999, p.45). But after Gayatri Chakravorty Spivak acknowledged the way in which the "silence" of the subaltern is dominated by "the ruling class 'in and by words' [*par la parole*]," the impact of "immaterial things" can no longer be denied (Spivak, 1988, p.68). Spivak had deftly conveyed the idea that when the subaltern has no voice or history, all that remains is biographical telling to ascertain subjectivity and agency. As this study on the (non-)speech act aims to show, judgments of speech and its legislation have great and formidable impact on the material lives of raced and immigrant subjects as intersectional subjects.

As such, this paper identifies, examines, and theorizes the (non-) speech act in three different ways. Firstly, the *institutional silencing* legislated by the Arizona House bill provides an educational example for exposing the judgments of accented speech as "defective" speech in the determination of racial difference. The silencing of "immigrant speech" is yet another method for surveilling the territorial borders that exclude the immigrant subject by discriminating against those deemed as un-American under the "illegal immigrant" stereotype. As Butler emphasizes, it is the "binding character of legal language" in the performance of laws delimiting the rights of a discriminated group that has the potential to "redouble that injury in the service of injustice." (Butler, 1996, p.216) Secondly, an examination of the strategy of *self-silencing* as a form of (non-)performativity of race and gender through the (non-)speech act reveals the impact of certain educational processes. The performance of self-silencing is a method of negotiating the institutional norm, particularly as a response to institutional silencing. In his 2007 autobiography, *My Grandfather's Son*, Justice Thomas reveals the way in which his own rural Southern speech was considered as defective speech by his high school teacher in Catholic school, a determination that affected his ability to speak thereafter in the classroom (and ostensibly on the Supreme Court bench much later) (Thomas, 2007). The biographical and the institutional provides a context for uncovering the silencing act, as confirmed by Thomas's explanation of his experiences growing up in all-white Catholic schools. The strategy of "keeping quiet" constitutes the instrumentalization of the silencing act, which secures the assigned place for people of color in exclusively white institutions. Lastly, the concluding examination of this paper looks to the expressive work of poetry that offers a method of resistance against repressions of accented voice. In the work of poet

Marilyn Chin, immigrant speech is valorized through the recognition and repetition of language, particularly when delivered through the oral tradition. Always biographical in its oral practice, poetry conceptualizes Austin's "doing things with words" in a way that elucidates the a priori condition of phenomenology in the speech act (Austin, 1962). As the vehicle for the poet's subjectivity and agency, Chin's performance functions as a feminist materialist model of empowerment for the female immigrant subject. As Coole and Frost argue, "materiality is always something more than 'mere' matter: an excess, force, vitality, relationality, or difference that renders matter active, self-creative, productive, unpredictable...a materiality that materializes, evincing immanent modes of self-transformation that compel us to think of causation in far more complex terms" (2010, p.9). Here, the practical phenomenology of poetry is contingent on the performance of the speaking poet who ultimately conveys the experiences of the material body, and in Chin's case, the Chinese female subject.

In the dynamic that can only be attested to by people of color, institutional silencing and self-silencing often does not appear to exist outside of personal experience, and the disavowal of difference remains the problem to overcome. Biographical testimony functions as the forum where the silences of the silencing act are broken in terms of providing evidence for the inherent biases of the institutional norm. Derrida's *Otobiographies,* his study on "'academic freedom,' the ear, and autobiography," is therefore useful for my analysis of accented speech and the (non-)speech act. Derrida's phenomenology of the "ear," presented in seemingly disparate contexts of academic freedom and autobiography, appears entirely cohesive and relevant through his review of Nietzsche's lecture *On the Future of Our Educational Institutions* (1872) – a work he describes as "a modern critique of the cultural machinery of the State and of the educational system" (Derrida, 1985, p.33). The biographical constitutes the difference between what is being said and the final determination of what is being heard in regards to accented speech as racialized speech. And as exemplified by Hill so long ago, autobiographical testimony continues to be the most prominent accounting of experiences of sexual or racial discrimination within the civic institution.

Institutional Silencing: Phenomenological and Juridical Acts

In her book *On Being Included,* Ahmed defines an activist process that "does not simply generate knowledge *about* institutions" but does so "in the process of attempting to transform them" (Ahmed, 2012, p.173). Ahmed's study acknowledges the phenomenological encounters that pertain to the specific experiences of women of color who must navigate within the academic institution. Her goal in understanding "institutions *as* formations" also distinguishes the aims for the first part of this essay, seeking to acknowledge and to comprehend the political function of institutional silencing (ibid., p.173). As shown by the case study of Arizona's targeting of the "immigrant accent" in association with Thomas's rural Southern accent impacting his high school experience, the judgment of racialized speech in the academic institution determines a far greater outcome for American society. The Arizona Department of Education's banning of Spanish-speaking teachers with "heavy accents" in 2010 was enacted under cover of the federal No Child Left Behind Act, and the new requirements for assessing English language fluency provided the reason for firing accented teachers who held positions in the schools (Jordon, 2010; Lavon Hanna and Allen, 2012). The policy is inseparable from the elimination of the voice given to Mexican-American history enacted by Arizona House Bill 2281, forbidding public schools from teaching certain materials focused on a particular ethnic group. The censuring of accented speech instantiates a significantly greater determination than just the surveillance of "correct English" within the academic institution. Rather, it substantiates the "defectiveness" of certain accents judged as inferior speech.

The important problem raised by Arizona's (non-) speech act is in legislating and confirming "defective" speech as a deliberation of the raced body as a whole, wherein accented speech is an extension of the "disfigurements" of skin. Rey Chow provides the illustrative example of the discrimination of the "brown and yellow offshore call-center agents" whose speech is inextricable from skin color: "is not the voice de facto an (objectified, artefactual) exterior and surface, not unlike the skin, on which is now inscribed an explicit demand, left over from an unequal historical relation?" (2014, p. 9) Chow goes on to question the rejection of the corporeality of these phone-representatives who "must adapt their bodies – the shapes of their mouths, their lips, their teeth, and their tongues as well as their vocal cords – to the manner of self-expression deemed acceptable by North American and other English-speaking customers, are not their skin tones also disfigurements, the defective corrections of what is already deemed defective?" (ibid.) The impact of this kind of judgment, also enacted by Arizona legislation, is especially detrimental to school-age students, particularly since it is administered by the state educational system. The institutionalizing of the non-accented norm is meant to reinforce the greater mandate for English-only rather than bilingual instruction in Arizona public schools.

This type of institutional discrimination is an insidious problem and its impact is hard to address. The measuring of the enforced silences of Mexican Americans, like the confirmation of absences, is not an action that can be verified when evaluating the educational system. Ahmed's metaphor for the institutional "brick wall" can elucidate the problem more clearly through the new materialist approach for making visible and physical the process of interpellation. Ahmed illustrates the instrumentality of the brick wall by acknowledging the material force of the otherwise invisible object of the social norm that people of color come up against: "(you are brown, stop!)"; but "to those who do not come against it, the wall does not appear – the institution is lived and experienced as 'yes' as being open, committed and diverse" (Ahmed, 2012, p.174). The invisible forms of oppression (deceptively untraceable) are rendered more tangible through the visualization of the wall, one that realizes the materiality of the (non-)speech act – the unspoken, "you are brown, stop," constitutes the object and aim of the embodied exchange of racism.

The overt legislation in Arizona exposes the silencing wall as one of many metaphorical and physical walls that police the borders of immigrant life. As verified in the aftermath of Arizona's enforcement of fluency standards, the legislated prohibition of accent is yet another form of political silencing that has little to do with education proper. Studies by linguists and social theorists have now shown that Arizona's initiative has no basis in measurable learning since there is no proven evidence that foreign accents can deter fluency in a particular language. More disturbing is the fact that the criteria itself for evaluating teachers for accent cannot be supported since there are no formal federal or state policies, no exact standards for evaluating teacher accent in relation to English fluency. As shown in the conclusive research by Patricia Lavon Hanna and Ann Allen (2012, p.718), the "ADE [Arizona Department of Education] has offered no clear explanation about why it interprets fluency as accent"; rather, the teachers had already proven their qualifications by passing the state's rigorous exams for educational licensing, completing preparatory programs, and achieving their degrees from accredited universities. The intelligibility of accented speech can only be judged subjectively but when considered in association with House Bill 2281, prohibiting the teaching of ethnic studies, Arizona's institutional silencing appears solely as racially determined. The act of silencing through the surveillance of Mexican-American speech appears to be used primarily as an instrument for maintaining political power.

Arizona's regulation of Mexican-American voice, speech, language, and history can therefore be construed as a concerted effort in the anti-immigration goal of policing state borders. In this way, the destinational structure of hearing erects a wall that might be as effective and more of a barrier than the 1.2 billion dollar, 700-mile double-layered fencing along the U.S.-Mexico border approved by Congress in 2006 (Weisman, 2006). In addition, the "virtual wall" of surveillance cameras, constructed and installed along the entire length of the Arizona border, was authorized as part of Homeland Security's Secure Fence Act. When President Obama declared the completion of the Secure Fence project in 2011, he forewarned that "Republicans would demand a 'higher fence' or a 'moat' with alligators in it" (*The Dallas Morning News*, 2011). Trump's 2016 campaign promise, promoting a "great, great wall" along the Mexican border, confirms Obama's prognosis of the Republican obsession. The act of silencing in Arizona schools is yet another method of wall-building, working to block the immigrant subject by legislating speech and mandating knowledge that conforms to dominant (white) social norms. Under the guise of assimilation, the objective is to subjugate students through this functionary mode, much in the way that Ahmed's metaphorical brick wall infers that being heard is dependent on the "person" of the institution (educational system/ state entity/social body), who comprehends, translates, and ultimately does the judging – "you are brown, stop!" The only testament to this exchange is the speaker who faces the wall of silence, which is actually a wall of conformity ensuring that no voice, no speech, no language, no history can be heard from the "undesirable" foreigner who does not belong in the United States.

This may seem to be an incredulous assertion but recent studies have shown that speakers with Latino and Asian accents are judged as less American than those with no accents or regional Boston or Southern accents. According to linguists John Dovidio and Agata Gluszek, discrimination toward specifically Latino and Asian speakers is distinguished by negative stereotypes associated with immigrant citizenship, ethnic nationalisms, and civic patriotism. Based on their research, biases against accented speech have *more* impact than raced appearances since "listeners discriminate against speakers with non-native accents in employment, housing, and the courts" (Dovidio/ Gluszek, 2010, p.73). The linguists conclude that while "there is clear evidence of negative attitudes (prejudice) and stereotypes toward Latinos, documentation of discriminatory behavior is rare," largely because participants of empirical studies "are often concerned about revealing their true underlying prejudice" (ibid., p.61). This kind of disavowal is yet another type of practice in the phenomenology of silencing that keeps the stereotype in place.

Among accents within the United States, Bostonian and Southern accents are no more comprehensible in different regions than Spanish accents in Arizona. Justice Thomas offers insight into his own educational experiences in high school, having to endure judgments of his "defective" rural accent from Pinpoint, Georgia. Recounted in his autobiography, *My Grandfather's Son*, Thomas was one of two African-American students admitted into the all-white seminary, Saint John Vianney, in Savannah, Georgia where he matriculated at sixteen years of age (Thomas, 2007, p.34). His recollection of perhaps his biggest influence, Father William Coleman, was most revealing: "Father Coleman told me matter-of-factly that I didn't speak standard English and that I would have to learn how to talk properly if I didn't want to be thought 'inferior'." (ibid., p. 34). As shown by his experience, Thomas's rural Southern accent was judged according to class distinctions for "educated English." But as asserted by linguists Tracy Derwing and Murray Munro, accent has more often than expected been "used as a cover-up for racism and other kinds of discrimination" (2009, p. 476). This form of discriminating by accent reveals how stereotypes are established through racially defined speech.

Dovidio and Gluszek (2010, p.73) point out that not all foreign voices are judged according to the "immigrant dialect" that signifies the status of the undesirable alien. The French accent for instance is never heard negatively as "alien" but always as romantic since accents are of course dependent on the listening ear. The singularity of the individual doing the hearing distinguishes the subjectivity of hearing, but overall, the discrimination of a singular speaking voice requires a broader social convention – a greater listening audience who determines "inferior" speech as in the political fate of Spanish accents in Arizona. Perhaps this is the reason why Derrida focuses on the "ear" of the other in his reading of Nietzsche, which, as Peggy Kamuf (2008, p. 182) noted in her analysis of *Otobiographies*, the philosopher went to "some lengths to avoid saying 'ears" conjecturing that "singularity points us in a different direction, toward a different difference." In other words, hearing by an *individual* will always be different from the social hearing of the *communal* ear.

In questioning the "hearing" of Nietzsche's *On the Future of Our Educational Institutions* - his warnings to his students about the apparatus of education and the state - Derrida suggests that what was spoken by Nietzsche was not the issue at all but the "destinational structure" of hearing that allows for "double interpretation and the so-called perversion of the text." (Derrida, 1985, pp.32-33) The philosopher was specifically addressing the fact that "the only teaching institution that ever succeeded in taking as its model the teaching of Nietzsche on teaching will have been a Nazi one." (ibid., p.24) Elsewhere, Derrida's *biographèmes* recounted his own "de-citizenships, ex-inclusions, blacklistings, doors slammed in your face" during his school-age years in Algeria under the Vichy disenfranchisement of the Jewish population (Cixous, 2004, p.5). Autobiography alone can confirm the discriminations that Derrida attributes to the misconstrual of Nietzsche's teachings, apparently by ordinary people in Germany. And whether or not the hearer hears a "defective" Jewish accent would have been an engagement of the destinational structure since the functioning "ear of the other" determines the outcome of judgments of racial difference (Derrida, 1985, p.21). To hear the Fascist message in Nietzsche's *On the Future of our Educational Institutions* becomes a warning that befits Arizona's (non-)speech acts against immigration. As Derrida argues, "today's teaching establishment perpetrates a crime against life understood as the living feminine: disfiguration disfigures the maternal tongue." (Derrida, 1985, p. 21) The example of Arizona's foreclosure of the living speech act perpetuates what Derrida characterizes as the "dead paternal language of the law," since his conception of "living speech" was connected to the treatment of the *mother-tongue* (in Derrida's use of the gendered vernacular), "as if it were a dead language and as if one had no obligation to the present or the future of this language." (Derrida, 1985, p. 21) The "ear of the other," according to Derrida, enables the performance of the "living ear" conceivable from the premise that "everything comes down to the ear you are able to hear me." (Derrida, 1985, p.4)

The axiom of "freedom of speech," however, marks the difference in the political economy of education in the United States. Inextricable from the tenets of American democracy, the censuring of speech – most visibly in the censorship of literature and art – would test the limits of freedom. Of course, the exception or contradiction can be found in the regulation of what can be spoken and taught in the classroom, which is usually viewed as an acceptable form of censorship under the rationale of the "moral" obligation to children under a certain age. Whilst the Supreme Court ruled favorably in 1985 on "the principle that individual instructors are at liberty to teach that which they deem to be appropriate in the exercise of their professional judgment," individual courts nevertheless consistently uphold the decisions of school boards and state administration policies in judicial cases involving banned materials (Sharp, 2012, p.4). Here precisely is what Derrida addresses as the use of "morality" in education through the concept of "degeneration," one that is perhaps easier to recognize in the Nazi denunciation of "degenerate art." The Fascist example is a clear misreading of Nietzsche's conception of the "degenerate," one in which Derrida had noted Nietzsche's frequent use of the word to characterize "notably university culture once it has become state-controlled and journalistic. This concept of degeneration has – *already*, you could say – the structure that it 'will' have in later analyses, for example in *The Genealogy of Morals*" (Derrida, 1985, p.27). The way in which "degenerate art" (the Nazi term *Entartete Kunst*) had come to mean exactly the opposite of Nietzsche's morality reveals the ruse of freedom under the discernment and regulation of the State. It is the logic of censorship bound to the concept of academic freedom that constituted the premise of Derrida's forewarning in *Otobiographies*. Fundamentally, he was questioning the function of the academic institution in the legislation of censorship under the political ruse of degeneracy.

The Instrumentality of Self-Silencing
as a (Non-)Speech Act

The flipside of institutional censorship is self-silencing, which could be defined as the response to experiencing censorship as an educational process. The potential outcome of the Arizona legislation prohibiting Spanish accents and Mexican studies is the self-silencing of students who must navigate within an Arizona community that disapproves of the tones of their "mother-tongue" as much as it censures the colonialist history of the conquest of Mexico. Derrida's analysis of the ruse of academic freedom was a warning against this very kind of instrumentalization of education, but his focus was also on the type of student that was produced by such a system. As the example, Justice Thomas is one who experienced the silencing of his rural Southern accent at school and is today known best for being silent on the Supreme Court bench. While Thomas provides a compelling explanation for why he kept quiet in the high school classroom, the lesser-known part of his biography is the extreme hardship he had to overcome as an African American. Growing up in the abject poverty of Georgia, his Catholic education was the foundation of his success in gaining entry to Yale Law School and then achieving confirmation as a Justice in the Supreme Court. Thomas's autobiographical subject presented in his own voice in *My Grandfather's Son* contends with his role as a Supreme Court Justice serving the Republican-party balance of political power as the second African American in history to have sat on the bench. Under the objective of perpetuating the institutional norm, it would seem that the instrumentality of self-silencing is more powerful than institutional silencing because it ensures that people of color maintain the existing hierarchy in exclusively white institutions. The way in which self-silencing works is through tacit forms of silencing overall.

The crux of Derrida's argument in *Otobiographies* could be understood by his acknowledgment of the historical impact of self-silencing as part of the educational process in maneuvering within the academic institution. Self-silencing only appears to be a quiet, passive and unassuming act since it functions to fulfill the specific character of the "functionary of the state," a role defined by Derrida as the figure "in the service of force, its docile instrument, servile and thus [thought to be] exterior to the dominant power." (ibid.) A docile, servile instrument offers up power implicitly to the ruling majority, and Derrida provided the example of the unquestioning members of the Gymnasium who would enable the most heinous crimes under "the ruse of the State, 'the most perfect ethical organism' (this is Nietzsche quoting Hegel)" and this ruse of academic freedom actually "conceals and disguises itself in the form of laisser-faire." (ibid., p.33) Derrida implicates the policy of non-interference as providing cover for highly political objectives in which the significance of the role of unquestioning functionaries cannot be overstated. Imposed as a priori condition of the institutional norm, the silencing act is an invisible act that is all the more powerful for its elusive recognizability.

The person of color serving as a state functionary fulfills a particular role since self-silencing is an act of agreement with the institutional norm. The embodied act of "keeping quiet and keeping your head down" (advice I have received on many occasions) secures this "rightful role" for people of color and actually protects their place in exclusive workplaces such as the sanctioned halls of the judiciary as the archetype for the upper echelons of academic institutions. Because he had for so long refrained from speaking on the bench, Justice Thomas appears to be the very model of this role since withholding from oral arguments since 2006. As a model for "difference that makes no difference," nothing exemplifies "no difference" more than the failure by one who represents difference to speak up from his highest position on the Supreme Court bench – a position made more significant since it was bequeathed by Thurgood Marshall, the first black Supreme Court justice. I have argued elsewhere that Thomas provides a model of *self-dismissal* that ensures the success of non-whites working in dominant white institutions because his strategy "enables a powerful outcome: the Supreme Court Justice title for a black male affects the balance of the conservative vote." (Chin Davidson, 2016) And thus, it is conceivable that through self-silencing Thomas fulfills his position in the highest judicial realm, the sovereign space that Hill was prohibited from entering after she was publicly dismissed for her personal testimony presented at the 1991 hearings.

But self-silencing is a coping mechanism, and Chow's analysis in her book *Not Like a Native Speaker: on Language as a Postcolonial Experience* traces the impact of the (non-)speech act on another prominent figure, President Barack Obama. Chow provides the example of the unforgettable experience that Obama included in his autobiography, recounting his visceral and painful reaction as a nine-year-old to a photograph of a black man undergoing chemical treatment to lighten his black skin: "As in a dream, *I had no voice* for my newfound fear." (Chow, 2014, p.7) Chow suggests that the young Obama was dumbstruck at the sight of the man's skin that "will forever bear the unattained *tones* of whiteness (the promise of happiness, as Obama points out), that preferred color, language, and voice with which it tries, in vain, at once to speak and hide itself." (ibid, p.8) The ability to overcome the impact of this "double disfigurement" – to rise above speechlessness and speak as the President of the United States – is to overcome *self-devaluation* based on skin "tones." As defined by Chow, the conflation of visual and audio significations of race proves the "irreducibility of language as a phenomenological actor," especially from experiences of childhood (ibid.).

In his autobiography, Thomas describes an experience similar to Obama's conflation of the tones of the skin and the voice, revealing the endurance of the phenomenological impact of the double disfigurement. Having attended Catholic high schools during the majority of his youth, Thomas discusses the insults he received from his fellow students prior to Saint John Vianney at St. Pius X, the only African-American Catholic high school in Savannah Georgia in the 1960s: "Most of the insults aimed at me had to do with the darkness of my skin, the flatness of my nose, the kinkiness of my hair, and the way I talked. (My speech was still full of the Geechee dialect I had grown up hearing in Pinpoint [Georgia] and from Daddy and Aunt Tina.) It was only adolescent hazing, but it still hurt." (Thomas, 2007, p.30) Taunted with the nickname "ABC-America's Blackest Child" at a time when calling a dark-skinned Negro 'black' was highly offensive, the racial slurs that came from his African-American classmates were the most injurious. But Thomas attributes his self-consciousness in speaking out loud in the classroom to his later experiences and Father Coleman's criticism at Saint John Vianney who told the sixteen-year-old that his inability to speak "standard English" would mark him as "inferior." Father Coleman had offered to help him improve his speech but Thomas felt his "blunt words hit me like a slap in the face." (ibid., p.34) The impact was much greater since Thomas credits his overall motivation to Coleman's hurtful judgments of inferior speech and his silencing act: "I vowed that day that no one would ever again say such things to me." (ibid.) The violence of "blunt words" obviously left their marks on Thomas's conception of the self, which not unlike Obama, biographically conveys the intellectual development of the first African-Americans in the highest leadership positions in the United States.

Thomas explains the difference, however, in his own management of race as an embodied subject who is distinct and separate from the speaking subject. The transformation came much later when he reviewed Coleman's criticism as a judgment of solely his inferior speech: "I thought he was saying that I was inferior because I was black"; however, "years later, I found out that he'd said similar things to white students whose accents were about as thick as mine – but his candor hurt me, and it also made me self-conscious about talking out loud in class." (ibid.) The important aspect of his autobiographical telling is the impact of the injury of his teacher's criticism and the acceptance of self-silencing as a compromise. His method of dealing with Coleman's judgment was through a disavowal of "race," divorced now from the pure "defectiveness" of his speech since the Father had also criticized white students as well. Thomas was able to rise out of his impoverished circumstances in rural Georgia by receiving a privileged education from Catholic schools. What the sixteen-year-old "heard" was a racial interpellation that would change his life forever, and yet his acquiescence to Coleman's silencing act would remain in the forefront of his role as the adult Supreme Court Justice. The formative event would establish Thomas's agreement with the institutional norm (an institution of theological and academic tradition), influencing a self-silencing that maintains a particular "difference that makes no difference." As the figure of authority, Coleman represents the Catholic school, which functions principally here as the system of education and the State.

As described by Chow, "even as one transcribes and expresses oneself through skin, as one must, it also wounds and humiliates one." (2014, p.6) Her analysis of the phenomenological condition of "aphasia or speech loss" attributes self-silencing to a "compulsory 'self' recognition" of race as disfigurement. At the mercy of the interpellation, as revealed by Fanon, this figuration is established by one's *reaction* to the 'dirty nigger' 'I'm frightened' speech act (ibid., p.6-7). The effects are interminable and inexplicable and to recount or narrate the past cannot quite illustrate the enduring sense-perceptions of violence felt in the present, although Thomas's description in his autobiography was quite effective. Self-silencing is a compromise and its counterpart is self-dismissal which requires the impossible confirmation of an "absence" much in the way that Spivak's "Can the Subaltern Speak" was a project of *"measuring* silences." (Spivak, 1994, p.66) This concept was also important to my other essay "Performative Testimony and the Practice of Dismissal" focusing on "dismissal" and "self-dismissal" in relation to the exclusion of raced subjects in the category of "woman" in Women's Studies (Chin Davidson, 2016). Only the autobiographical can account for the non-hirings, the refusals of tenure, and the day-to-day dismissals of women of color in their experiences as teachers in the university. The "dismissed" woman of color can be viewed in clear contrast to those who we have seen follow the model of docility and self-imposed silence in order to maintain their positions in the academic institution.

Poetic Speech Acts of Resistance

The limitations of the temporal "time" of autobiography which, as intimated by Derrida, is to think of "the writing of life by the living" or essentially the experience of the "time of life's *recit*" which is always in the rear view without much effective self-agency for the present (Derrida, 1985, p.11). In discussing the experience of self-silencing with a close South Asian colleague, I was reminded of the profound effect of my own "immigrant dialect" when we were reminiscing about learning to speak English. Impossible to acknowledge is the response to the immigrant voice that cannot be heard except by those who experience the wall of silencing, and we hear it loud and clear: "*you don't belong here.*" As children of parents who emigrated to the United States when we were both very young, we shared similar experiences in our role as the family mouthpiece, speaking on behalf of parents whose lack of English proficiency and thick Asian accents kept them in an incomprehensible space. My own self-silencing began with the terror I felt at nine-years-old, translating for my mother at the grocery counter, a fear that ended at fifteen when it was replaced by the anger I felt toward the grocery clerks who stared in hateful disdain when my grandmother spoke too loudly at the same grocery counter. To this day, I know this disdain without someone so much as uttering a word to me, and it took a long time to recognize the self-hatred that comes with the shame of the immigrant accent, because, of course, our nine-year-old translations were just as incomprehensible to the ear of the other.

The expressive work of poetry can better elucidate through words the affective sense of "life by the living"; in particular, the poetry of Marilyn Chin who captures poignantly the dynamic of the immigrant accent. In her anthemic poem *How I Got That Name: an Essay on Assimilation*, Chin uses the auto-biographical form to establish the poetic power of the speaking subject through proclaiming her name out loud: "I am Marilyn Mei Ling Chin/ Oh, how I love the resoluteness/ of that first person singular/ followed by that stalwart indicative."(Chin, 1994, p.16) The poem goes on to acknowledge her mother's failure to speak her English name with the immigrant accent: "My mother couldn't pronounce the 'r' / She dubbed me 'Numba one female offshoot'/ for brevity: henceforth, she will live and die; in sublime ignorance." (ibid.) In my personal reading of this poem, Chin is articulating the powerful sense of self-alienation that the immigrant accent can instill in girlhood. The poetic use of the word "ignorance" can be read as the difference between the child's vulnerability to being viewed as "ignorant" and the child's wish that her mother could bypass her humiliation – a "sublime ignorance" suggests the mother is unaware of her "inferior" speech. In Chin's poetic acknowledgement, accented speech becomes a powerful form of expression since it communicates beyond or as a supplement to actual words. In a controversial passage of *Otobiographies,* Derrida explains that there is a "law that creates obligations with regard to language, and particularly with regard to the language in which the law is stated: the mother tongue. This is the living language (as opposed to Latin, a dead, paternal language, the language of another law where a secondary repression has set in – the law of death)." (Derrida, 1985, p.21) Seemingly essentialist in this gendering of language, Derrida invokes the "ear attuned to the name of the dead man and the living feminine"; however, the point of the passage is his focus on the patronymic "name of my death, of my dead life" in reference to the institution of archaic legacies contained within language itself (ibid.). In contrast, he attributes to the feminine the "living ear" that hears the spoken word, not the written text.

The reader of Chin's poem can grasp the lyricism of her testimony through the written word; however, the engagement of the actual political critique becomes particularly effective when the poet delivers her testimonial "first person, stalwart indicative" from the commanding position of the speaking subject. In his book titled *Foreign Accents,* literary critic Steven Yao acknowledges Chin's expression as "lyric testimony" since the poet "persistently and unapologetically [pursues] a 'political' agenda" shared amongst Asian-American writers who confront subjects of "dominant racism, immigration, minority or 'ethnic' identity, and gender oppression." (Yao, 2010, p.187) Chin is well known for her oral delivery since she is a poet in great demand for her poetry readings. As an artistic experience, the spoken word is regarded as phenomenologically separate from textual production, since audio comprehension is a temporal activity in the present that is remarkably different from the cognition of the written message. The phenomenological domain of the oral in relation to the literal has long been associated with oral poetry. Words themselves are represented visually only through writing, otherwise they are spoken as sound.

The special relationship between spoken sound and the objects they represent is found in the transcendent meaning that occurs from the engagement between speaker and listener. Oral poetry is "intellectualized mnemonically," suggests Walter Ong, since it conveys meaning through the specific power of its "event" for the greater community (Ong, 2002, p.31). Ong's seminal study of oral cultures reveals how the "the writing of life by the living" was originally conducted only through the spoken word which is exemplified most clearly by the poetic speech of the Homeric tradition. In Chin's model of *political* engagement descending from this cultural tradition, the orality of poetry provides yet another way to understand the phenomenology of the speech act as *a form of resistance*. Chin's overt scheme of political enunciation espouses and extends the ritual authority of the longstanding oral tradition. But when presented by the embodied Chinese woman poet herself, the power of the speech act and the delivery of the first-person naming – "I am Marilyn Mei Ling Chin" – incites a rupture to the patronymic textual tradition of naming considered by Derrida as the "name of the dead."

A poetic performative can function in this way to illustrate Ahmed's explanation that "a performative acquires force only through citation and repetition; A non-performative speaks to a gap between the past and future tense. The speech act is a commitment that points to the future it brings about…but the past that accumulates overrides this futurity, as what the institution is committed to, by sheer force of habit."(Ahmed, 2012, pp.126-27) The assertions of a brown woman speaking subject on the public stage is still something of an event.

However, the repetition of the (*non-*)speech act, the passive and quiet non-performative, has become the force of habit that tends to overrule the power of the singular performative act. Any radical change is incumbent on leadership to give voice and to propose action on a greater social scale within the given institution. But as explained by Ahmed, the "barrier to change" is only felt by the discriminated, and because it "remains invisible to those who can flow into the spaces created by institutions," it is a material condition for only a particular contingency (ibid., p.175). The endeavor to make visible this barrier that is invisible to those in power is the most important objective for disrupting the silencing act in the institution. As people of color attain high-ranking positions, their acknowledgment of the "immaterial things" such as their own self- silencing acts can determine the material future for the greater whole. As Ahmed forewarns, the (non-)speech act of "getting people to the table by not speaking of the wall (by not speaking about what does get across) does not mean the wall disappears." (ibid.) But should it ever occur that people actually speak about the wall of silence or its implied issues, the outcome will always be contingent on the habits of the listening ear of the other.

References

Adewunmi, B. (2014, April). Kimberlé Crenshaw on intersectionality: "I wanted to come up with everyday metaphor that anyone could use." *New Statesman*. http://www.newstatesman.com/lifestyle/2014/04/kimberl-crenshaw-intersectionality-i-wanted-come-everyday-metaphor-anyone-could

Ahmed, S. (2000). *Strange encounters: Embodied others in postcoloniality*. London: Routledge.

Ahmed, S. (2012). *On being included: Racism and diversity in institutional life*. Durham: Duke University Press.

Ahmed, S. (2014). *Willful subjects*. Durham: Duke University Press.

Ahmed, S., & Fortier, A.M. (2003). Re-imagining communities. *International Journal of Cultural Studies, 6*(3), 251-259.

Austin, J.L. (1962). *How to do things with words*. Oxford: Clarendon Press.

Barad, K. (2003). Posthumanist performativity: Toward an understanding of how matter comes to matter. *Signs: Journal of Women in Culture and Society, 28*(3), 801-831.

Butler, J. (1988). Performative acts and gender constitution: An essay in phenomenology and feminist theory. *Theatre Journal. 40*(4), 519-531.

Butler, J. (1996). Burning acts: Injurious speech. *University of Chicago Law School Roundtable*, 3 (1), 199-221.

Chow, R. (2014). *Not like a native speaker: On language as a postcolonial experience*. NY: Columbia University Press.

Chin Davidson, J. and Reddy, D. S. (2016). Performative testimony and the practice of dismissal. In P.A. Matthew (Ed.), *Written/unwritten: Diversity and the hidden Truths of tenure* (pp. 127-147). Chapel Hill: University of North Carolina Press.

Chin, M. (1994). *The Phoenix gone: The terrace empty*. Minneapolis: Milkweed.

Cixous, H. (2004). *Portrait of Jacques Derrida as a young Jewish saint*. New York: Columbia University Press.

Cohen, A. (2013, January). Speak, Clarence, speak! *Atlantic*. http://www.theatlantic.com/national/archive/2013/01/speak-clarence-speak/267169/

Coole, D. & Frost, S. (Eds.) (2010). *New materialisms: Ontology, agency, and politics*. Durham: Duke University Press, pp. 1-41.

Crenshaw, K. (1991, July). Mapping the margins: intersectionality, identity politics, and violence against women of color. *Stanford Law Review*, 43(6), pp. 1241-99.

Derrida, J. (1985). *Otobiographies: The teaching of Nietzsche and the politics of the proper name*. (P. Kamuf, Trans.). NY: Schocken Books.

Derrida, J. (1992). Force of law: The 'mystical foundation of authority. In D. Cornell, M. Rosenfeld, D.G. Carlson (Eds.), *Deconstruction and the possibility of justice*. NY and London: Routledge, pp.3-67.

Derwing, T. & Munro, M. (2009, Oct.). Putting accent in its place: Rethinking obstacles to communication. *Language Teaching*, 42 (4), pp.476-490.

Dovidio, J.F. & Gluszek, A. (2010). Understanding bias toward Latinos: Discrimination, dimensions of difference, and experience of exclusion. *Journal of Social Issues*, 66 (1), pp.59-78.

Fraser, N. (1990). The uses and abuses of French discourse theories for feminist politics. *boundary 2*, 17(2), pp.82-101.

Gabbatt, A. (2015, Jun 16). Donald Trump's tirade on Mexico's "drugs and rapists" outrages US Latinos. *The Guardian*. https://www.theguardian.com/us-news/2015/jun/16/donald-trump-mexico-presidential-speech-latino-hispanic. Accessed 11 December 2016.

Hennessy, R. & Ingraham, C. (1997). *Materialist feminism: A reader in class, difference, and women's Lives.* NY and London: Routledge.

Jordan, M. (2010, April 30). Arizona grades teachers on fluency. *Wall Street Journal.* http://www.wsj.com/articles/SB10001424052748703572504575213883276427528

Kamuf, P. (2008, Spring). The Ear, Who? *Discourse,* 30(1/2), pp. 177-90.

Landry, D. & MacLean, G. (1993). *Materialist feminisms.* Cambridge: Blackwell.

Lavon Hanna, P. & Allen, A. (2012). Educator assessment: Accent as a measure of fluency in Arizona. *Educational Policy,* 27(4), pp. 711-738.

Liptak, A. (2013, Jan. 14). Justice Clarence Thomas breaks his silence. *The New York Times.* http://www.nytimes.com/2013/01/15/us/clarence-thomas-breaks-silence-in-supreme-court.html

McGough, M. (2014, Feb. 21). Justice Clarence Thomas' silence is "disgraceful"? Not really. *Los Angeles Times.* http://www.latimes.com/opinion/opinion-la/la-ol-clarence-thomas-supreme-court-silence-20140221-story.html

Nussbaum, M.C. (1999, Feb.22). The professor of parody. *The New Republic,* pp. 37-45.

Ong, W. (2002). *Orality and literacy.* NY: Routledge.

Sharp, R. (2012). Point: academic freedom: should k-12 teachers have greater control of the content of the curricula they teach? In C. J. Russo (Ed.) *School Law* (pp. 4-11). Thousand Oaks: Sage   Publications.

Spivak, G.C. (1994). Can the Subaltern Speak? In P. Williams & L. Chrisman (Eds.) *Colonial discourse/Post-Colonial Theory: A Reader* (pp. 66-111). NY: Columbia University Press.

The Dallas Morning News. (2011, May 21). Fact Check: Republicans Who Deem Border Fence Inadequate Should Put Part of Blame on Hutchison, http://www.dallasnews.com/news/local-politics/2011/05/21/fact-check-republicans-who-deem-border-fence-inadequate-should-put-part-of-blame-on-hutchison

Thomas, C. (2007). *My grandfather's son.* NY: Harper Collins.

Toobin, J. (2013, Jan. 14). Clarence Thomas speaks, finally. *The New Yorker.* http://www.newyorker.com/news/news-desk/clarence-thomas-speaks-finally

Weisman, J. (2006, Sept. 30). With senate vote, congress passes border fence bill. *The Washington Post.* https://www.washingtonpost.com/archive/politics/2006/09/30/with-senate-vote-congress-passes-border-fence-bill-span-classbankheadbarrier-trumps-immigration-overhaulspan/5f52efd4-05d5-4c1b-98a6-edc776a1bbc6/?utm_term=.8b55d72c6847

Yao, Stephen. (2010). *Foreign Accents: Chinese American verse from exclusion to postethnicity.* Cambridge: Oxford University Press.

Review of *Theorizing NGOs: States, Feminisms, and Neoliberalism*, edited by Victoria Bernal and Inderpal Grewal, Duke University Press, 2014. 379 pp., $27.95 (cloth)

Reviewed by Rachel Denney
University of Kansas

Theorizing NGOs: States, Feminisms, and Neoliberalism combines cutting-edge feminist research on non-governmental organizations (NGOs) and how they have affected the conditions of women's lives and feminist movements. Using an intersectional feminist perspective, Victoria Bernal and Inderpal Grewal, the editors of the anthology, argue that the NGO label has become too broad, causing everything that is good about NGOs to be lumped in with the bad and masking the wide variation in form and function across the non-governmental sector. Bernal and Grewal contend that NGOs have come to be defined by what they are not – namely, not the state. While celebrated by some, this juxtaposition has been criticized by some authors in this collection. Borrowing from Foucault, Bernal and Grewal propose that NGOs have become a parallel form of governmentality, which makes them a conduit for advancing "neoliberal projects of privatization and state withdrawal" (p. 8). The authors argue that NGOs have become gendered in ways that mirror the division between the masculine public sphere of governance and the feminine domestic sphere of care work.

Theorizing NGOs focuses on the uneasy relationship between feminist theory/practice and the NGO sector. Many critics have argued that NGOs have appropriated feminist language to further their own, non-feminist – or at least, less radical – agendas. This is reflected in Sabine Lang's piece on the European Union and the de-politicization of feminist movements. Others have extended this argument to claim that NGOs are pushing Western feminist norms, while ignoring the political, economic, and social realities of local women. This was the theme of Elissa Helms's chapter on women's organizing in Bosnia-Herzegovina, where women's social groups resisted the "feminist" label while simultaneously pushing for gender equality on the local level. Finally, scholars like Laura Grunberg, while acknowledging some of the problematic elements of the NGO model, still insist that productive work can be accomplished by this form of activism.

The volume consists of eleven chapters divided into three sections, in addition to an introduction and conclusion by Bernal and Grewal. The first section, "NGOs Beyond Success or Failure," looks at the relationship between the state, civil society, and NGOs. The chapters in this section all demonstrate the complications of working both with and against state structures and competing understandings of gender, agency, and citizenship. The second section, "Postcolonial Neoliberalisms and the NGO Form" examines NGOs in the wider global context and their potential to re-inscribe power hierarchies related, but not limited, to gender, class, North-South, and rural-urban relations. This section also critically examines the much-lauded microcredit phenomenon, showing that it is not always a panacea. The final section, "Feminist Social Movements and NGOs," discusses how feminist movements have been both challenged and, in some instances, strengthened by the transnational spread of NGOs. Again, this section points to the need for nuance in analyses of NGOs and feminism, resisting an all-encompassing narrative. Saida Hodzic makes this point particularly well in her chapter, which argues that the "master narrative" of feminists rallying against the specter of neoliberalism actually masks the diversity of women's movements and romanticizes a history of feminism that may have never existed.

One of the most satisfying elements of this collection is its diversity of geographic representation. Bernal and Grewal include pieces that represent almost every region of the world, from Europe to Asia to Latin America. Much of the literature on NGOs suffers from being either an overly-specific qualitative ethnography or a wide-ranging, yet shallow, quantitative analysis. Placing the pieces together in an anthology like this one allows the authors to situate their particular case studies in context. While this sheds light on unique challenges in each locale, it also confirms existing patterns in the NGO literature, namely the conflict between foreign donors and local NGO staff/clients, the misfit of liberal "global" (aka Western) norms with on-the-ground realities, and the compulsion to throw good money after bad – that is, to fund projects long after they have ceased to be effective.

This is not to say that every author in this anthology negates the value of NGOs. To the contrary, many confirm that NGOs are often the only ally of marginalized groups, such as Aradhana Sharma's piece on the state and women's empowerment in India. In her chapter, she shows how a government-organized NGO (GONGO) – a novel hybrid structure – used its connections and institutional knowledge to assist rural women in fighting government corruption and suppression of their land rights. Lauren Leve's work on Nepalese female sympathizers with Maoist revolutionaries shows how a rural literacy program helped women develop political consciousness, though perhaps not in the way that international donors may have intended. Finally, Sonia Alvarez revisits the Latin American feminist backlash against NGOs in the 1990s, showing how blanket condemnations of NGOs masked the ways they are able to agitate for feminist goals and disseminate previously subjugated knowledges. The alternative – and even conflicting – viewpoints represented in this anthology further confirm the need to question how the scholarship engages with NGOs.

Theorizing NGOs adds a critical piece to the literature on NGOs by addressing the implications for feminism and the gendered nature of NGOs themselves. While many studies of gender and NGOs solely examine these organizations' impacts on women, this anthology addresses the way new gendered subjects are produced through the process of NGO-ization. This work resists sweeping conclusions and, instead, argues for a nuanced look at the process of interaction between states, feminisms, and NGOs, and is a worthwhile read for scholars of feminist theory, NGOs, and civil society.

Review of *Buying a Bride: An Engaging History of Mail-Order Matches* by Marcia A. Zug, New York University Press, 2016, 320 pp., $30.00 (cloth)

Reviewed by Skye de Saint Felix
University of Arkansas at Fayetteville

Working to combat "simplistic and inaccurate" (p. 1) conceptions of mail-order brides as helpless, desperate, and abused victims, Marcia A. Zug uses *Buying a Bride: An Engaging History of Mail-Order Matches* as a textual intervention into dominant U.S. cultural narratives, which she argues are tainted with misconceptions and moral judgements about this practice. In this text, Zug traces the history of mail-order brides in America from 1619 in the Jamestown colony to present times in order to address the balance of risk and reward associated with mail-order marriages. By focusing on how these marriages have historically been empowering arrangements that have helped women escape servitude while affording them economic benefits, greater gender equality, and increased social mobility, *Buying a Bride* articulates a forgotten record of women's liberation. This text also examines the role of whiteness, and xenophobia in fostering attitudes of intolerance and animosity, which work in tandem to perpetuate inaccurate narratives which associate this practice with violence, subservience, and human trafficking.

The Introduction begins by questioning dominant cultural assumptions about mail order marriages and develops the author's central thesis that mail-order marriages have had and continue to have significant benefits for both men and women in the United States. To evidence this argument, the book is divided into two sections to highlight a post-Civil War ideological shift that transformed mail-order marriages from an empowering to an oppressive concept. Part I, "When Mail-Order Brides Were Heroes," charts the antebellum belief that such arrangements were crucial to a thriving society. Part II, "Mail Order Marriage Acquires A Bad Reputation," outlines the culture of disdain, skepticism, and criticism that developed toward this practice and continues to mask its potential benefits. The clear sections of the book demonstrate the changing perceptions of not only these arrangements, but also of love, gender, and marriage in general.

Chapter One, "Lonely Colonist Seeks Wife," discusses how the U.S. practice of mail-order marriages began in the Jamestown colony as a means to encourage men to marry, reproduce and contribute to colonial success. As many European women refused to immigrate for fear of experiencing famine or disease, the nascent colonial government began to encourage mail-order arrangements to deter marriage between white settlers and indigenous women. Many mail-order brides were awarded monetary compensation and received greater legal, economic, and property rights than they could have in seventeenth century England, and hence made rational, calculated decisions to immigrate. This chapter clearly emphasizes the benefits of mail-order marriage, but it significantly downplays how these arrangements affected indigenous peoples; Zug only briefly mentions that mail-order marriage was used by colonial governments to "displace Indian people and acquire Indian lands" (p. 29).

Chapter Two, "The Filles du Roi," and Chapter Three, "Corrections Girls and Casket Girls," highlight how the colonies esteemed whiteness, discouraged marriage between indigenous women and white settlers, and justified government interference in immigration policies that transported white women to America. Chapter Three is the only section of her book to consider potential downfalls of this practice through an examination of the traffic in women to the Louisiana colony, to which many French women convicted of theft or prostitution were sent and forced into marriage with white settlers. Zug asserts that this practice reflected government policy and hence cannot truly be considered a mail-order marriage practice. This chapter is key in examining the detrimental effects of forced migration while exposing the crucial role whiteness played in justifying and encouraging these practices to the colonies. Chapter Four, "Well Disposed Toward the Ladies: Mail-Order Brides Go West," addresses mail-order marriage in mid-nineteenth century California and the Pacific Northwest. Zug describes such marriages as a solution to the need for labor that provided women with greater freedom through liberal property and divorce laws.

Part II of the book traces how mail order marriage practices began to acquire a negative reputation after the Civil War. Chapter Five, "Advertising for Love: The Rise of Matrimonial Advertisements," demonstrates that although the practice became more widespread and women began to have more control over the entire process, popular culture in the U.S. and U.K. continued to negatively depict advertising for spouses. Chapter Six, "Wanted—Correspondence," discusses the post-Civil War shift in the marital landscape that enticed more women, especially women of color, to enter into mail-order marriage. This occurred as part of a broader trend in which the U.S. state and local governments made only limited efforts to promote mail-order marriages after a given area reached its demographic goals. Meanwhile, public discourse focused on this practice's perceived dangers, iterating stories of murder, theft, fraud, and forceful seduction and downplaying its benefits to men, women, and the nation. This chapter illustrates a crucial shift in the acceptance of mail-order marriage as it transformed from a "mixed reputation to outright hostility" (p. 156), once women of color became the primary practitioners of this arrangement.

Chapter Seven, "Marriage at the Border," expands on this premise, arguing that relations between migrant women and women born in the United States grew increasingly hostile after the passage of the Expatriation Act (1907), which granted women citizenship upon marriage to an man who held U.S. citizenship. Women who were not U.S. citizens were perceived by some U.S. women as an obstacle to domestic feminism. Such opposition and disdain further demonized the practice as evidenced through public dialogue from journalists, such as Natalie De Bogory, that described mail-order marriages as loveless arrangements that ensure female subservience and act as "death sentences to individuality and progress" (p. 183).

In the 1950s "golden age" of marriage, when marriage rates increased and people began to marry much younger, mail-order marriages were widely regarded as unnecessary and outdated. Feminist texts such as Betty Friedan's *The Feminine Mystique* (1963) prompted women to reconsider their notions of happiness and marriage and to advocate for increased access to education, civil rights, abortion, and birth control. Chapter Eight, "Mail-Order Feminism," concludes the author's history of mail-order marriages in the United States by arguing that the practice is still very much alive today, with more than 400 marriage broker agencies currently in operation (p. 189). To adjust to contemporary technology, websites are charging for things like video chats and emoticons, expenses that perpetuate the conception that men are "buying" brides. In light of its popularity, Zug argues that texts such as Mila Glodava and Richard Onizuka's *Mail Order Brides: Women for Sale* (1994) exaggerate and misinterpret domestic violence rates for mail-order marriages while literature such as Lynn Visson's *Wedded Strangers* (1998) reinforces negative stereotypes of men who seek mail-order brides as pathetic and misogynistic.

This text is an important intervention raises critical questions about the role of whiteness, xenophobia, and government in shaping the practice of mail order marriage. Although some information is repetitive, the book provides detailed historical and personal accounts, including a myriad of testimonies from individuals who have been part of mail order marriages. The author juxtaposes this data with analyses of legal and popular cultural discourse from newspapers, scholarship, films, and legislation that shaped, and were shaped by, migration associated with mail-order marriages. In tracing the transformation of the practice from one regarded as rectifying gender disparities within settler colonialism to the contemporary perspective of mail order marriage an impediment to gender equality, *Buying a Bride* works to critically engage with popular cultural perspectives on these arrangements. By describing women as the "biggest beneficiaries of mail-order marriage" (p. 207) Zug accentuates how she views these practices as having feminist potential.

The book sometimes suffers from an intensely positive and optimistic tone, with only one chapter that provides a negative account of mail-order marriages, which makes the author's argument appear narrow and one-sided. In so doing, the author omits aspects of mail-order marriages that deserve further investigation, such as the effect mail-order marriages had on indigenous peoples during colonial times or international perceptions of its practice in the United States. Similarly, Zug concludes her work by using marriage equality as a platform to define modern marriage by choice, not love. While I find it encouraging that she included the recent popularity of mail-order practices to help same-sex couples find one another, her consideration appeared as a quick afterthought for her arguments.

Zug is careful to note that she does not suggest that mail-order marriages should become a dominant standard in U.S. society, but rather that the practice be analyzed according to its potential and its extensive history which has always carried risks and uncertainties. These consensual arrangements can offer significant economic, social, and legal benefits for women, and hence this book plays a crucial role in engaging with the intersections of feminism, imperialism, capitalism, and racism that inform the conflicted history of mail-order marriages in the United States.

www.ingramcontent.com/pod-product-compliance
Lightning Source LLC
Chambersburg PA
CBHW030440290526
45786CB00001B/382